Job Interview Questions Series

C000111185

CORE JAVA

INTERVIEW QUESTIONS
YOU'LL MOST LIKELY BE ASKED

367
Interview Questions

VIBRANT
PUBLISHERS

CORE JAVA

INTERVIEW QUESTIONS
YOU'LL MOST LIKELY BE ASKED

Paperback ISBN 10 :   1-63651-040-X
Paperback ISBN 13 :   978-1-63651-040-8
Ebook ISBN 10:   1-63651-041-8
Ebook ISBN 13:   978-1-63651-041-5

Library of Congress Control Number: 2021938075

Vibrant Publishers books are available at special quantity discount for sales promotions, or for use in corporate training programs. For more information please write to **bulkorders@vibrantpublishers.com**

Please email feedback / corrections (technical, grammatical or spelling) to **spellerrors@vibrantpublishers.com**

To access the complete catalogue of Vibrant Publishers, visit **www.vibrantpublishers.com**

TABLE OF CONTENTS

Section 01: Core Java

Section 02: Java 8

TABLE OF CONTENTS

Dear Reader,

Thank you for purchasing **Core Java Interview Questions You'll Most Likely Be Asked.**
We are committed to publishing books that are content-rich, concise and approachable
enabling more readers to read and make the fullest use of them. We hope this book provides
the most enriching learning experience as you prepare for your interview.

Should you have any questions or suggestions, feel free to email us at
reachus@vibrantpublishers.com

Thanks again for your purchase. Good luck with your interview!

– Vibrant Publishers Team

OOPs Concepts

001. Explain method overloading and method overriding

Answer:

Method overloading occurs when there are two or more methods in a class with the same name but with different number/type of arguments.

The following code demonstrates this:

```
public class Calculator {
    public int add (int a, int b) {
        return a+b;
    }
    public double add (double a, double b) {
        return a+b;
    }
    public int add (int a) {
        return a+a;
```

```
        }

}
```

Method overriding occurs when there is a method in a sub–class that has the same name and number of arguments as a super–class method.

The following code demonstrates this:

```
public class Animal {
      public void saySomething () {
            System.out.println("I am an animal");}

      }

}
public class Dog extends Animal {
      public void saySomething () {
            System.out.println("I am a dog");

      }

}
```

002. Explain the benefits of OOPs.

Answer:

Following are the benefits of OOPs:

a. **Reusability** – OOPs principles like Inheritance, Composition and polymorphism help in reusing existing code.

b. **Extensibility**– Code written using OOPs principles like Inheritance makes code extensible

c. **Security** – OOPs principles like encapsulation help to keep the data and the code that operates on the data together and makes the code secure

d. **Simplicity** – Java classes represent real world objects. This makes code very easy to understand

e. **Maintainability** – Code written using OOPs principles is easier to maintain

003. Write a code snippet that demonstrates encapsulation.

Answer:

Encapsulation refers to keeping the data and the code that operates on the data together as a single unit. Simply creating a class with private fields and public getter/setter methods is an example of encapsulation.

The following code snippet demonstrates this:

```
public class Laptop {
    private String memory;
    public String getMemory () {
        return memory;
    }
    public String setMemory (String newMemory
    {
        memory = newMemory;
    }
}
```

Here, there is a class called `Laptop`. It has a private field called `memory` and public getter and setter methods to access/modify the `memory` field. So, the `memory` field cannot be accessed directly outside the class, it can only be accessed via its getter/ setter methods.

004. What are the types of inheritance relationships?

Answer:

Inheritance relationships specify how code can be reused. There are two types of inheritance relationships. They are as follows:

a. IS–A

An IS–A relationship is implemented via inheritance, that is by creating a sub–class. Assume that, `Camera` is a subclass and `Electronics` is a super class. In that case, we can say that, `Camera` IS–A `Electronic` product.

b. HAS–A

A HAS–A relation can be created via composition, that is by creating a field corresponding to another class. Assume that, inside the `Camera` class, there is an object called `Battery`. In that case, we can say that `Camera` HAS–A object called `Battery`.

005. What is the best practice in declaring instance variables?

Answer:

Instance variable should always be declared as private. They should have public getter/setter methods. This helps to protect the instance variable as they can only be modified under the programmer's control. This is as per the Encapsulation principle.

Declaring instance variables as public violates the encapsulation principle and poses a security issue. Public instance variables can be maliciously modified outside your class. If at all an instance variable needs to be accessed from a sub–class, it can be made protected.

006. What is a singleton class?

Answer:

A class which lets you create only one instance at any given time is termed a Singleton class. A Singleton class can be implemented via a private constructor and a public getter method.

The following code demonstrates this.

```
public class MySingleton {
   private static MySingleton mySingletonInstance;
   private MySingleton () {
   }
   public static MySingleton getInstance () {
      if (mySingletonInstance == null) {
         mySingletonInstance = new MySingleton (); //
create the object only if it is null
      }
      return mySingletonInstance;
   }
   public void doSomething () {
      System.out.println("I am here....");
   }
   public static void main(String a[]) {
      MySingleton mySingleton = MySingleton.
      getInstance();
      mySingleton.doSomething();
   }
}
```

Here, a private constructor and a public getInstance method is defined. The getInstance checks if an instance exists. If an instance does not exist, it creates one using the private constructor. If an instance exists, it just returns it. Any external class that needs an instance of the Singleton class, needs to obtain it via the getInstance method. The getInstance method ensures that there is only one instance of the Singleton class.

007. Explain what happens when the following code is compiled and state whether it uses method overloading or overriding.

```
class Electronics {
public void displayPrice (Float price) {} //Line 1
}
class Camera extends Electronics {
   public void displayPrice (String price) {} //Line 2
}
```

Answer:

The above compiles fine. It uses method overloading. `Camera` is a sub–class of `Electronics` and both classes have a method called `displayPrice`. However, the `displayPrice` method in both classes differ in the type of argument.

008. Write a Java code sample that demonstrates method overloading

Answer:

Method overloading occurs when there are two or more methods in a class with the same name but with a different number/type of arguments.

The following code demonstrates this:

```
class Laptop {
   public void displayPixel (int width, int height) { };
   //Line 1
   public void displayPixel (float width, float  height)
   {}; //Line 2
}
```

The class Laptop has two method with the name as `displayPixel`. The `displayPixel` method at Line 1 has two arguments, both of type int. The `displayPixel` method at Line 2, `displayPixel` method has two arguments both of type float. So here, the `displayPixel` method is said to be overloaded

009. What is polymorphism? How does Java support Polymorphism?

Answer:

Polymorphism literally means "many forms". It is the ability to use the same interface to execute different code. Java achieves polymorphism via method overloading and method overriding. Method overloading occurs when there are many methods in a class with the same name but different number/ type of arguments. The version of an overloaded method that will be invoked is determined at compile time based on the number/type of arguments passed in. Method overriding occurs when a sub–class has a method with the same name and type signature as a method in the super class. The version of an overridden method that will be invoked is determined at run time based on the type of object that invokes the method.

010. Explain how Java achieves abstraction

Answer:

Abstraction is an OOPs concept whereby only the necessary information is exposed to the end user and the internal implementation details are hidden. Java achieves abstraction via abstract classes and interfaces. So, you can declare the methods that you want to be exposed to the outside world in an abstract class or interface. The actual implementation will be within concrete classes that extend the abstract classes or implement the interfaces. The outside code is not aware of the implementing classes, they interact with your code via the interfaces or abstract classes.

This page is intentionally left blank

Java Basics

011. What are the possible ways of declaring the Java main method?

Answer:

Following are the possible ways of declaring the Java main method.

```
a. public static void main (String argument
   [])

b. static public void main (String argument
   [])
```

So, while declaring the Java main method, the order of the public, static, void keyword does not matter, they can be written in any order.

012. What are the possible ways of declaring a Java class?

Answer:

Following are the possible ways of declaring a Java class:

```
a. public class Class1 {}

b. class Class2 {}

c. private class Class3 {}

d. protected class Class4 {}

e. static class Class5{}
```

Approach a declares a class as `public`. **Approach b** does not use any access specifier, so it has default access. It will be accessible only within the package. **Approaches c & d** use the `private, protected` access specifiers. Note that a high–level class cannot have these specifiers. This can only be used for an inner class. **Approach e** uses the static keyword. Again, only an inner class can have this access specifier.

013. How will you define an Identifier?

Answer:

Identifier is the name given to a class, method or variable or interface. There are several rules for Java identifiers. These are as follows:

- Identifiers must start with an alphabet, the dollar sign ($), or an underscore character (_)

- Identifiers can contain alphabets, digits, $ and _

- Identifiers cannot contain special characters

- Identifiers are case sensitive

Some of the examples of legal identifiers are shown below:

- b
- $a
- book
- author1
- myName
- ___1_c

014. What are the modifiers that cannot be specified with an instance variable?

Answer:

The following modifiers cannot be specified with an instance variable:

a. **Abstract** – is valid only for classes, interfaces and methods, it cannot be specified with an instance variable

b. **synchronized**

c. **native**

The keywords synchronized and native are valid only for methods and cannot be specified with an instance variable.

d. **void** – can only be specified as a return type, when a method does not return any value.

015. What are the modifiers that can be specified with a method declaration?

Answer:

The following keywords can be specified with a method declaration:

a. **public**

b. **private**

c. **protected**

The keywords **public, private** and **protected** are access specifiers. They specify from where the method can be accessed.

d. **static** – used to indicate that the method is a class level method

e. **final** – used to indicate that the method cannot be overridden.

f. **abstract** – used to specify that a sub–class should override the method

g. **native** – used to specify that the method is implemented in another language like C++

h. **synchronized** – used to indicate that the method can be accessed by only one thread at a time.

016. What will be the default value of a reference variable when it is not explicitly initialized? How will you handle this in code?

Answer:

When a reference variable is not explicitly initialized, then its value is null by default. If such variables are not properly handled, they can result in a `NullPointerException`. So, in order to avoid the `NullPointerException`, you can do one of the following:

• Ensure that variables are properly initialized

• Explicitly add null checks in your code

• Use Java 8 Optionals.

017. Explain the keywords "transient" and "native"

Answer:

The keyword **transient** can be used as a modifier for an instance variable. It specifies that the JVM should ignore the variable while serializing the containing object.

The keyword **native** can be used as a modifier with methods. It specifies that the method is implemented in another language like C, C++.

018. What is a comment in Java? Explain the types of comments supported by Java

Answer:

A comment is some text added to the code that provides additional information about the code. It describes what the code does to the readers of the code. Comments are ignored by the compiler. Java supports 3 types of comments as follows:

a. **Single Line Comment** – Such a comment begins with two forward slashes (//) and ends at the end of the line. The following code snippet demonstrates this:

```
int count; // This stores the number of objects
```

b. **Multi Line Comment** – This starts with /* and ends with */. Anything between these two is treated as a comment and ignored by the compiler. The following code snippet demonstrates this:

```
/*
This for loop repeats a block of code 10 times
*/
for (int i=0; i < 10; i++) {
}
```

c. **Documentation comment** – Documentation comments are comments that are used to generate documentation for the code via the JavaDoc tool. They start with /** and end with */. The following code demonstrates this:

```
/**
* Method that does something
* @param a
*/
public void myMethod (int a) {
}
```

019. Explain what is JVM, JRE and JDK

Answer:

JDK stands for Java Development Kit. It consists of the tools and libraries that are required to write and run a Java program. So, it includes the Java compiler, JRE and other tools.

JRE stands for the Java Runtime Environment. It consists of the tools that are required to run a Java program. It is included with the JDK but it can also be installed by itself. If the JRE is installed by itself without the JDK, you will be able to run a Java program but you will not be able to write and compile Java code. JRE includes the JVM and some other libraries.

JVM stands for the Java Virtual Machine. Java code is compiled into byte code. This byte code is executed within the JVM. So, the JVM just provides an execution environment to execute code.

020. Explain with a code sample how you will read a value entered by a user

Answer:

Java provides a class called `java.util.Scanner`. This can be used to read an input from a user. The following code demonstrates this:

```
System.out.println("Enter a Number:");
Scanner scanner = new Scanner (System.in);
int num = scanner.nextInt();
System.out.println("The entered number is "+num);
scanner.close();
```

This code creates a `Scanner` corresponding to `System.in` which is the standard input. It then asks the user to input a number and reads this number into the variable `num` via the `scanner.nextInt` method. So, this code prints the following output:

```
Enter a Number:
10
The entered number is 10
```

Just like `nextInt`, the `Scanner` class has several other methods that can be used to read data of different types like `String`, `float`, `long`, `boolean`, etc.

This page is intentionally left blank

Data Types, Variables and Arrays

021. What are the possible ways of declaring an array of short data type?

Answer:

You can declare an array of short data type in any of the following ways:

```
a. short a1[];
b. short [] a2;
c. short b1[] [];
d. short [] [] b2;
e. short [] c1 = {2,3,4};
f. short c2[] = {2,3,4};
```

Approaches **a** and **b** declare a single dimensional short array.

Approaches **c** and **d** declare a two–dimensional short array. Approaches **e** and **f** declare a single dimensional short array and initialize it. In all the approaches, the square brackets can be placed either after the variable name or after the short keyword.

022. How will you cast an int variable to byte explicitly? Is it really necessary to cast int literal to byte?

Answer:

An int variable can be cast to byte as follows:

```
int i = 30;
byte bValue = (byte)i;
```

So, you need to specify the "byte" keyword before the int variable. Yes, it is necessary to cast an int variable to byte explicitly, otherwise a compilation error will occur as below:

```
byte bValue = i; //compilation error
```

This is because int is a wider type as compared to byte. So, Java cannot automatically convert the int type to byte, you need to specify an explicit cast.

023. Give an example of implicit casting.

Answer:

Implicit casting occurs when a value is assigned to a variable of a wider data type. In such cases, the conversion happens by default and there is no need of an explicit cast. For example, if you assign an int value to a long value, an implicit cast will occur. The following code snippet demonstrates this:

```
int iValue = 250;
```

```
long lValue = iValue;
```

The above code explains that an int value can always be assigned to a long variable without casting and the conversion happens by default.

024. Write a code snippet that demonstrate how you can assign a float value to a short variable

Answer:

The following code demonstrates converting a float value to a short variable:

```
float fValue = 37000.02F;
short sValue = (short) fValue;
```

Here, the keyword short is specified before the float variable fValue, this is known as explicit cast. Since float is a wider data type than short, an explicit cast is required.

025. What is the default value for int, double, float, boolean, long and char data types?

Answer:

The default values for the data types mentioned above are as follows:

```
int = 0
double = 0.0d
float = 0.0f
boolean = false
long = 0L
char = 'u0000'
```

026. In the following code snippet, explain which lines will compile fine and which will cause a compilation error

```
int [] [] add = new int [2] []; //Line 1
int [] subtract = new int [2]; //Line 2
int iValue = 2; //Line 3
add[1] = subtract; //Line 4
add[1] = iValue; //Line 5
```

Answer:

Line 1 compiles fine as it creates a two–dimensional array. Line 2 compiles fine as it creates a single dimensional array. Line 3 compiles fine as it declares and initializes an int variable. Since a two– dimensional array is an array of arrays, Line 4 also compiles fine. It assigns a single dimensional array to one of the dimensions in the two–dimensional array. Line 5 causes a compilation error because we cannot assign an int variable to an int array variable.

027. Explain what happens when the following code is compiled

```
public class Car {
    public Car (String carName) {}
}
Car myCar = new Car("Benz");
Car [] myCars = { myCar, new Car("Ford"), new
Car("BMW")};
```

Answer:

The code compiles fine, there is no issue at all. The code first creates a Car class. It creates a car object called myCar. Finally, it creates a Car array called myCars which is initialized with three values. The Car constructor is directly invoked during array initialization.

028. You are given an assignment to create a game of Tic Tac Toe using a multi–dimensional array. Which of the following is the correct way to initialize the array?

```
a) int ttt   = new int[3][3];
b) int[]ttt  =new int[3][3];
c) int[][]ttt  =new int[3][3];
d) int ttt  [3][3]=new int[][];
```

Answer:

(c) Answer c is correct. The correct syntax for declaring a multi–dimensional array is

```
int[][]ttt  =new int[3][3];
```

029. Explain the primitive data types in Java

Answer:

There are eight primitive data types in Java. These are as follows:

Name	Width (Bits)	Range
byte	8	–128 to 127
short	16	–32,768 to 32,767
int	32	–2,147,483,648 to 2,147,483,647
long	64	–9,223,372,036,854,775,808 to 9,223,372,036,854,775,807
float	32	1.4e–045 to 3.4e+038
double	64	4.9e–324 to 1.8e+308
char	16	0 to 65536
boole–an	1	true/false

030. What are the possible ways to assign a decimal number to a float variable?

Answer:

The following are the ways in which a decimal number can be assigned to a float variable:

```
float fValue1 = 100.5f;
float fValue2 = 100.5F;
float fValue3 = (float) 100.5;
```

A decimal number is treated as a double by default. So, in order to assign it to a float variable, it needs to be either followed with '**f**' or '**F**' or it should be explicitly be cast as a float type.

031. Identify the error in the following code snippet and explain how it can be fixed

```
byte bValue = 10; //line 1
bValue = bValue + 10; //line 2
```

Answer:

The above code will cause a compilation error at line 2. Line 2 assigns an int value to a byte variable and produces an int result. So, when the int value is assigned to the byte variable bValue, it causes a compilation error. This code can be fixed by specifying an explicit cast as follows:

```
bValue = (byte) (bValue + 10);
```

032. How will you assign an Octal and Hexadecimal literal to an "int" variable?

Answer:

Octal and Hexadecimal literals can be assigned to an int variable as follows:

```
int iValue1 = 0100;
int iValue2 = 0xf1dead;
```

An Octal literal need to be prefixed with '**0**'. Octal values can only use the digits 0–7

A Hexadecimal literal need to be prefixed with '**0x**' Hexadecimal values can use the digits 0–9 and the characters A, B, C, D, E, and F.

033. In the code snippet below, which lines will compile and which will cause an error?

```
char cValue1 = '@'; //Line 1
char cValue2 = '\u004E'; //Line 2
char cValue3 = 80000; //Line 3
char cValue4 = (char) -100; //Line 4
char cValue5 = 128; //Line 5
```

Answer:

Except Line 3, all lines will compile. Line 3 causes a compilation error because the range of character is from 0 to 65,536. In order for the line 3 to compile we have to modify the line as below:

```
char cValue3 = (char) 80000;
```

034. What happens when the following code is compiled and executed?

```
int [] iArray = new int[5];
int iInt = -5;
iArray[iInt] = 5;
```

Answer:

The code above compiles fine but on execution it will throw an `ArrayIndexOutofBoundsException`. This is because `iInt` is a negative number which cannot be used as an array index.

035. Consider the following code snippet and explain its output

```
public class ArrayDec {
    public static void main (String argv[]){
        ArrayDec ad = new ArrayDec ();
        ad.arrayMethod();
    }
    public void arrayMethod () {
        int intArr1[]= {1,2,3};
        int[] intArr2 = {1,2,3};
        int intArr3[] = new int[] {1,2,3};
        System.out.print(intArr3.length);
    }
}
```

Answer:

The code above compiles fine and produces the output 3. Since all the array declarations are correct, the code compiles fine. It prints the length of the `intArr3` which is 3.

Operators

CHAPTER

04

036. In the code snippet below, which lines will cause a compilation error and why?

```
String str = "Hello";
long lng = 99;
double dbl = 1.11;
int i = 1;
int j = 0;
j = i << str; //line 1
j = i << j; //line 2
j = i << dbl; //line 3
j = i << lng; //line 4
```

Answer:

Line 1 and Line 3 will cause a compilation error because they use incompatible primitives. Line 1 uses the << with an int and a String value whereas Line 3 uses the << operator with an int and double value.

037. What will be the output of the following code and why?

```
int x = -1;
x = x>>>24;
System.out.println(x);
```

Answer:

This code prints 255

Here, x is set to −1, which will set all 32 bits to 1 converting into binary. The value is then shifted right by 24 bits, filling the first 24 bits with 0s, not considering the sign extension. This sets x to 255.

11111111 11111111 11111111 11111111 represents −1 in binary >>>24

00000000 00000000 00000000 00000000 is the binary version of 255

038. Explain the operator available for string concatenation with a code sample.

Answer:

The '+' operator when used with Strings can be used for String concatenation. The following code demonstrates this:

```
String sum = "one" + "two";
```

In the above code, the Strings one and two are concatenated and assigned to the String object sum.

039. What will be the output of the following code?

```
public class Test {
    public static void main (String argument[]) {
        String name = "Java";
        int iInt1 = 100;
        int iInt2 = 200;
        System.out.println(name + iInt1 +
        iInt2);
    }
}
```

Answer:

The above code compiles fine and produces the following output:

```
Java100200
```

Since the '+' operator is used with a String and int variables, the final value is considered as a String and the values are concatenated and displayed.

040. Explain the % operator

Answer:

The % operator is called as the modulus or remainder operator. It returns the remainder obtained after dividing the number on the left with the number on the right. The following code demonstrates this:

```
100 % 4 //produces 0
10 % 4 // produces 2
```

041. What will be the output of the following code?

```
final int iIntFinal = 100;
int iValue = iIntFinal ++;
System.out.println("The output is:
"+iValue);
```

Answer:

The code will cause a compilation error. This is because the code tries to increment the final variable iIntFinal using the increment operator. A final variable cannot be modified. The code will work fine if the final variable is simply assigned to the iValue variable.

042. Explain what happens when the following code is compiled and executed?

```
int iValue = 100;
if(iValue = 100) { //line 1
    System.out.println("iValue is : "+iValue);
}
```

Answer:

The above code will cause a compilation error. At line 1, the assignment operator = is used and not the comparison operator ==. So, this assigns the value 100 to the variable iValue and produces an int result. The if condition cannot operate on an int value, it requires a boolean value to test.

043. Will the below code compile? If so, what will be the output?

```
int [] iArray = new int[10];
if(iArray instanceof Object) { //Line 1
    System.out.println("Object");
}
else
{
    System.out.println("int");
}
```

Answer:

The above code compiles fine and it displays the following output:

```
Object
```

An array is an object instance. So, when line 1 is executed, the if condition returns true.

044. What will be the output of the following code?

```
int iValue = 10;
int jValue =20;
if(iValue && jValue) { //line 1
    System.out.println(True will be printed...");
}
else {
    System.out.println("False will be printed...");
}
```

Answer:

The above code will cause a compilation error at line 1. The && is the logical AND operator and can only have boolean operands. It cannot be used with int values.

045. What will be the output of the following code and why?

```
System.out.println("Output is "+ ((10 <
100) ^ (100 > 10)));
```

Answer:

This code produces the following output:

```
Output is false
```

The reason is:

`10 < 100` returns true which can be denoted as 1

`100 > 10` returns true which can be denoted as 1

The XOR operation is applied on these values. The XOR operator returns 0 when both values are the same, otherwise returns 1. Since both values are true, the XOR operator returns 0 which corresponds to false

046. What will be output of the following code snippet? Explain the reasons

```
if(!(100 == 1000)) { //line 1
    System.out.println("TRUE gets printed");
}
else {
    System.out.println("FALSE gets printed");
}
```

Answer:

This code produces the following output:

```
TRUE gets printed
```

Line 1 checks the condition `100 == 1000`, which is false. The if statement checks the logical NOT(!) of this. The Logical NOT operator returns the opposite value of its operand. So, it returns a true. So, the if condition evaluates toa true and the output above is printed.

047. Explain the increment and decrement operators

Answer:

The increment operator is represented by two plus signs. It increments its operand. The following code demonstrates this:

```
int i = 10;
i++; // sets i to 11
```

The decrement operator is represented by two minus signs. It decrements its operand by 1. The following code demonstrates this:

```
int i = 10;
i--; // sets i to 9
```

048. Explain the instanceOf operator

Answer:

The `instanceOf` operator can be used to check if an object is an instance of another class. It returns a boolean value. If both the objects being compared are of same type it returns true and otherwise it returns false. The following code demonstrates this:

```
String str = "Hello";
str instanceof String //returns true
String str = null;
str instanceof String //returns false
```

049. Explain the ternary operator with a code sample.

Answer:

The ternary operator is also called as a conditional operator. It is a short cut operator for the if–else statement. Its syntax is as follows:

```
condition?TruePath:FalsePath
```

It evaluates a condition and if true, it executes code after the "?" symbol. If false, it executes the code after the ":" symbol. The following code demonstrates this:

```
int iValue1 = 100;
int iValue2 = (iValue1 == 100) ? 200 : 100;
//Line 1
```

Here, the `iValue==100` condition is evaluated. Since is it true, the value **200** will be assigned to the variable `iValue2`.

Control
Statements

050. Name the decision statements used in Java.

Answer:

Decision statements evaluate an expression and based on the result, performs the execution. There are two decision statements in Java. They are:

a. **if** – The **if else** is a conditional branch statement. It tests a condition and if the condition is true, execution follows a certain path and if not, it follows a different path. It has the following syntax:

```
if(condition){
    //some code here
}
else { // this part is optional
    //some code here
```

}

b. **switch** – The switch statement is a multi–way branch statement. It can be used instead of using several if else statements. The expression specified within the switch statement is evaluated and matched with every case value. Once a match is found, the code within the body of that case statement is executed. It has the following syntax:

```
switch(expression) {
    case value1:
        //some code
        break; //optional
    case value2:
        //some code
        break; //optional
    .....
    case valuen:
        //some code
        break; //optional
    default:
        //some code
        break; //optional
    }
}
```

051. What are the looping constructs in Java?

Answer:

Looping constructs are also known as iteration statements. They can be used to repeatedly execute a block of code. Java has the following looping constructs:

a. **while** – The while checks a condition and repeats a block of code as long as the condition is true. Its syntax is as follows:

```
while (condition){
    //body of the loop
}
```

b. **do while** – A do–while loop also repeats a block of code as long as a condition is true but it checks the condition at the end of the loop, so the body of the loop is executed at least once. Its syntax is as follows:

```
do{
    //body here
} while(condition);
```

c. **for** – A for loop can be used to iterates over a range of values. It continues the iteration until a condition is true, after which the loop is exited. Its syntax is as follows:

```
for(initialization;condition;iteration){
    //body of the loop
}
```

d. **for each** – The for–each loop is used to cycle through an array or a collection of objects. In each iteration of the loop, it fetches the next element from the array or collection and executes the body of the loop for that element.

```
for(datatype var : collection) {
    //body of the loop
}
```

052. Explain the syntax of the if–else statement with an example

Answer:

The following is an example of an if–else statement:

```
int iValue = 10;
if(iValue > 1000) {
System.out.println("iValue is > 1000");
}
else {
System.out.println("iValue is < 1000");
}
```

The if statement needs to be followed by a condition. If
the condition evaluates to true, the code following the if
statement is executed. If the condition evaluates to false,
the code following the else keyword is executed. Here, the
variable iValue has the value **10**, so the condition within the
if statement evaluates to **false** and so the code within the else
block gets executed. So, this code prints the following output:

```
System.out.println("iValue is < 1000");
```

053. Which of the following lines of code will compile and which will cause an error?

```
int iValue=5;
while (iValue) {} //Line 1
while (false) {} //Line 2
while (iValue = 5) {} //Line 3
while (iValue == 5) {} //Line 4
```

Answer:

Line 1 will cause an error because an integer value cannot be
passed to a while loop. It requires a boolean value.

Line 2 compiles file since the boolean value false is used in
the while loop

Line 3 causes a compilation error since the expression
iValue=5 does not evaluate to a boolean value, it is an

assignment statement

Line 4 compiles file since the expression `iValue==5` evaluates to a boolean value.

---

054. What would be the output if boolA is false and boolB is true?

```
public void foo( boolean boolA, boolean boolB) /*
Line 1 */
{
   if(boolA ) {/* Line 3 */
      System.out.println("X"); /* Line 5 */
   }
   else if(boolA && boolB) {/* Line 7 */
      System.out.println( "X && Y"); /* Line 9 */
   }
   else { /* Line 11 */
   if ( !boolB ){ /* Line 13 */
      System.out.println( "notY") ; /* Line 15 */
   }
   else{ /* Line 17 */
      System.out.println( "In here" ) ; /* Line 19
      */
   }
   }
}
```

Answer:

Output: In here

Since `boolA` is false, line 5 will never execute and **X** will not be printed. Since `boolA` is false line 7 will also not execute and so **X && Y** will also not be printed. The else block at line 11 will be entered. Since `boolB` is true, the if statement at line 13 is not executed. So, the else statement at line 13 is executed which prints `In here`.

055. What will be the output of the following program?

```
public class SwitchDemo
{
    final static short caseVal = 2;
    public static void main(String [] abc)
    {
      for (int iterNo=0; iterNo  < 3; iterNo ++) {
         switch (iterNo) {
             case caseVal: System.out.print("a ");
             case caseVal -1: System.out.print("b ");
             case caseVal -2: System.out.print("c ");
         }
      }
    }
}
```

Answer:

Output: c b c a b c

Since `caseVal` is declared as a final variable, it is evaluated at compile time. When `iterNo` = 0, the 3rd case statement is true, so it prints **c**. In the second iteration, `iterVal` becomes **1**, so the second case statement is true so it prints **b**. Since there is no break statement after the second case, the third case statement is also executed which prints **c**. During the third iteration, the first case is true and so all a is printed. This is followed by **b** and **c** since there is no break after case.

056. What happens when you execute the code below? If it compiles, what will be the output?

```
int iValue1 = 100;
int iValue2 = 200;
boolean isTrue() {
    return true;
}
if(((iValue1 > iValue2) && (iValue2 < 50))
|| isTrue()) { //Line 1
    System.out.println("This is True");
}
else {
    System.out.println("This is False");
}
```

Answer:

The code compiles fine and displays the following output:

```
This is True
```

The if statement at Line 1 uses an OR operation. An OR operation returns true when any one of its operands is true. Since the isTrue() method returns a true, the if statement will return a true. So irrespective of the result of the AND operation, the expression within the If statement returns a true.

057. What is the use of "break" and "continue" statements?

Answer:

The **break** keyword can be used within a loop. When the break statement is encountered, the loop is immediately terminated and control is transferred outside the loop.

The **continue** keyword can also be used within a loop. It is used to stop executing the next statement in the loop for the current iteration and transfer control to the start of the loop.

058. What happens when you compile and execute the code below? What will be the output?

```
for(int iValue=0; iValue<5; iValue++) {
    System.out.println(iValue); //line 1
    continue; //line 2
    System.out.println(iValue + 1);
}
```

Answer:

The code compiles and on executing it displays the below output:

```
0
1
2
3
4
```

After the Sysout statement at line 1, the continue statement at line 2 gets executed. This keeps the rest of the body of the loop and transfers control to the start of the loop.

059. What happens when you compile and execute the code below? What will be the output?

```
for(int iValue=0; iValue<5; iValue++) {
    System.out.println(iValue);
    break;
    System.out.println(iValue + 1);
}
```

Answer:

The code compiles and on executing it displays the following output:

0

It prints just 0. This is because the break statement stops executing the next statement in the loop and transfers control out of the loop.

060. What happens when you compile and execute the code below? What will be the output?

```
for (;;) {
    System.out.println("Will this get printed?");
}
```

Answer:

The above code compiles fine. However, it executes an infinite loop since there is no loop control variable and no condition to check. So, this code will keep on printing the output **"Will this get printed?"**.

061. What happens when you compile and execute the code below? What will be the output?

```
int iValue = 50;
for (;iValue < 100;) {
    System.out.println(iValue);
}
```

Answer:

In the above code, there is no initialization statement and iteration statement, it only specifies a condition. So, the variable iValue is never incremented. So, this becomes an infinite loop; it infinitely prints the value "50".

Output:

50

50

50

...

062. Give some examples of "for–each" loop

Answer:

The following are some examples of for–Each loop:

Example 1:

```
Integer [] integerArray = {10, 100, 1000};
for(Integer integer : integerArray) {
// do something here
}
```

Example 2:

```
int [] iValue = {10, 100, 1000};
for(int iValue1 : iValue) {
// do something here
}
```

Example 3:

```
Electronics [] electronics = {new Camera(), new
Laptop()};
for(Electronics e : electronics) {
// do something here
}
```

Example 4:

```
List<Integer> numbers = Arrays.asList(4,10,12);
for(int num : numbers) {
// do something here
}
```

063. What will be the output of the following code?

```
for(int iValue = 0; iValue < 10; iValue++) {
}
System.out.println(iValue);
```

Answer:

This code will not compile. This is because the scope of the variable iValue is only within the for loop and not beyond the for loop.

064. What will happen when you execute the code below? If it compiles fine, what will be the output?

```
int iValue = 10;
switch(iValue) {
    case 5: System.out.println("5");
    case 8: System.out.println("5");
    default: System.out.println("This is Default");
    case 9: { System.out.println("9"); break; }
    case 11: System.out.println("11");
}
```

Answer:

This code compiles fine and displays the output below:

```
This is Default
9
```

Although case 10 is not available, "default" gets executed. Since there is no break statement, the case statement following default also gets executed and prints 9. The code does not print 11 since there is a break statement after case 9.

Classes and Methods

065. Consider the following code snippet:

```
static void main(String argument[]) {
System.out.println("This gets printed");
}
```

What will be the output when this code is compiled and executed?

Answer:

The above code compiles fine. But on executing, an error occurs as follows:

```
Error: Main method not found in class
```

This is because the main method does not have the public access specifier, so it is not accessible outside the class. So, the JVM is not able to access the main method and the error occurs.

066. Can an instance variable be declared as static? Explain.

Answer:

An instance variable cannot be declared as static. If an instance variable is declared as static, then that variable becomes a class variable.

067. Explain what happens when the following code is compiled and executed.

```
class Laptop {
    Laptop(String laptopName) {
        System.out.println("Laptop Name is ....");
    }
    public static void main(String argument[]) {
        Laptop l = new Laptop();
    }
}
```

Answer:

The code will not compile and it will cause the following compilation error:

```
"The constructor Laptop() is undefined."
```

This is because there is no default constructor defined in this code. Since there is a constructor with argument, Java cannot automatically create a default no argument constructor. In order for this code to work, an explicit constructor needs to be added as follows:

```
Laptop() {
}
```

068. What happens behind the scenes if a constructor is not explicitly specified?

Answer:

If a constructor is not explicitly specified, the compiler automatically generate a default no arguments constructor. Whenever a new object is created, this default constructor is used.

069. Explain what happens when the following code is compiled

```
class Electronics {
Electronics() {
}
public void displayPrice() {
     Electronics();
   }
}
```

Answer:

On compiling the above code, it causes a compilation error `The method Electronics() is undefined for the type Electronics`. This is because it is illegal to call a constructor like this.

070. What are the possible access specifiers for a constructor?

Answer:

Below are the possible access modifiers for a constructor:

a. **private:** This denotes that the constructor is accessible only from its class

b. **public:** This denotes that the constructor is accessible from any class which resides in any package

c. **protected:** This denotes that the constructor is accessible from any class which resides in the same package

071. What will be the output of the following code snippet?

```
public class MyClass {
    public void callMe(int a) {
        System.out.println("Call me with int argument");
    }
    public void callMe(long a) {
        System.out.println("Call me with long argument");
    }
    public static void main(String args[]) {
        MyClass myClassObj = new MyClass();
        int i = 6;
        myClassObj.callMe(i);
    }
}
```

Answer:

The above code will print the following output:

```
Call me with int argument
```

Since the method `callMe()` is invoked with an integer value, the method that accepts an integer argument gets invoked. If we change the datatype of `i` to `long`, then the method that accepts a `long` type of argument gets invoked.

072. How will you define a constructor? Give an example.

Answer:

Constructor is a special method which has the same name as the class name but with no return type. The constructor is invoked automatically whenever a new object is created. It is most commonly used to execute some code that needs to be run as soon as an object of a class is created like setting initial values to the instance variables.

The following code demonstrates this:

```java
public class Electronics {
    int price;
    Electronics(int price) {
        this.price = price;
    } //constructor
    public static void main(String argument[]) {
        Electronics e = new Electronics(); //Line 1

    }
}
```

In the above code, as soon as Line 1 is executed, the JVM invokes the constructor. This initializes the price field with the value passed in.

073. Explain the void keyword with a code sample

Answer:

The void keyword is useful when a method does not return a value. It is specified as the return type for such methods. The following code demonstrates this:

```java
public void doSomething(){
}
```

Here, the void keyword is specified with the doSomething() method which indicates that this method does not return any value.

074. Explain the differences between a constructor and an ordinary method

Answer:

There are several differences between as constructor and an

ordinary method. These are as follows:

a. A constructor has the same name as the class name, an ordinary method can have any name

b. A constructor does not have a return type, not even void. A method has a return type. If a method does not return any value, then the keyword void needs to be specified

c. A constructor is automatically invoked when an object of the class is created. A method needs to be invoked explicitly

d. If a class does not have a constructor, Java automatically creates a default constructor. If a class does not have a method, Java does not automatically add a method

075. Explain this keyword with a code sample

Answer:

The this keyword is used to refer to the current object. It can be used to reference a field or a method corresponding to the current object. The following code demonstrates this:

```java
public class Book {
    private String name;
    private String author;
    public Book(String name,String author) {
        this.name = name;
        this.author = author;
    }
    public void doSomething(Book book) {
    }
    public void doSomethingElse(Book book) {
        this.doSomething(book);
    }
}
```

This code creates a class called Book. It has a constructor that initializes the name and author fields. The this keyword is used to refer to the current object's copies of the name and author fields. This helps in distinguishing between the instance fields and the variables passed in. The this keyword can also be used with methods. So, the doSomethingElse method invokes the doSomething method via the this keyword.

076. Explain the differences between a class and an object

Answer:

There are several differences between class and an object. These are as follows:

a. A class acts like a template and defines a new data type. An object on the other hand is a value of that data type

b. A class does not have any memory allocated to it. An object has memory allocated to it

c. A class is a logical entity, an object has physical existence

d. A class is declared using the class keyword, an object is created using the new keyword

e. A class does not have a state, an object has state

077. Explain the new keyword with a code sample

Answer:

The new keyword is used to allocate memory for an object. It needs to be followed by a call to the constructor of the method. The following code snippet demonstrates the new keyword:

```
Person person1 = new Person();
```

Here, Person is the name of the class, person1 is an object of type `Person`. The `new` keyword is followed by the constructor for the `Person` class. This allocates memory for the `person1` object. The `new` keyword is only required to be specified with objects and not for primitive types like int, double, etc.

078. What will be the output of the following code snippet?

```
public class MyClass2 {
    private int field1 = 0;
    private static int field2 = 0;
    public static void main(String[] args) {
        MyClass2 object1 = new MyClass2();
        object1.field1++; //Line 1
        object1.field2++; //Line 2
        MyClass2 object2 = new MyClass2();
        object2.field1++; //Line 3
        object2.field2++; //Line 4
        System.out.println(object2.field1); //Line 5
        System.out.println(object2.field2); //Line 6
    }
}
```

Answer:

This code will print the following output:

1

2

Here, the class `MyClass2` has 2 fields, `field1` and `field2`. `field1` is an instance field while `field2` is a static field. When it comes to instance fields, each object of a class has its own copy of instance fields. So `object1` and `object2` will have their own copies of `field1` and Lines 1 and 3 will cause this copy of the field to be incremented. However, in the case of static fields, there is only one copy of the static fields corresponding to all the objects of the class. So, there is only one copy of `field2` corresponding to `object1` and `object2`. So, lines 2 and 4 will increment this same copy and cause Line 6 to print the value 2.

079. Explain the return keyword with a code sample

Answer:

The return keyword is used at the end of a method to return a value which is the result of some computation. The value returned must match the return type of the method. The following code demonstrates this:

```
public int add(int num1,int num2){
    int sum = num1+num2;
    return sum;
}
```

This method has an int return type. It returns the sum of addition.

Even if a method does not return anything, the return keyword may optionally be specified without any value. The following code demonstrates this:

```
public void printSum(int a,int b) {
    int sum = a+b;
    System.out.println(sum);
    return;
}
```

In this case, the method has a `void` return type which indicates that the method does not return anything. However, the return keyword is still specified.

Inner Classes

080. What is an inner class? What are the different types of inner classes?

Answer:

An inner class is any class defined inside the body of another class. There are 4 types of inner classes as follows:

a. **Nested class** – Class is defined within the body of another class. It has access to all the members of the outer class.

b. **Static nested class** – A nested class that is static is known as a static nested class. It cannot access non–static members of the outer class.

c. **Method local inner class** – A class that is defined inside a method of another class is known as a method local inner class. Such an inner class can only access final members of the outer class.

d. **Anonymous inner class** – A class that has no name and can be instantiated only once when it is defined is known as an anonymous inner class. It does not have a constructor as it does not have a name. It cannot be static. The class definition ends with a semicolon.

081. Write a code sample that demonstrates how you can instantiate an inner class from an outer class

Answer:

Suppose you has an outer class called `TestOuter` with an inner class called `TestInner`. The following code snippet demonstrates how you can instantiate the `TestInner` class:

```
TestOuter outer = new TestOuter();
TestOuter.TestInner inner = outer.new
TestInner();
```

So first, you need to create an instance of the outer class. Since the inner class is a member of the outer class, you can then create an instance of the inner class by using the dot operator(.). Also, while invoking the inner class constructor with the new operator, you need to specify the outer class object instance with the dot operator.

082. Write a code sample that demonstrates an Inner Class.

Answer:

The following code demonstrates an inner class:

```
class Outer {
    private int iValue = 100;
    public void callInner() {
        Inner inner = new Inner();
        inner.readValue();
```

```
    }
  class Inner {
    public void readValue() {
       System.out.println("Value is : " + iValue);
    }
  }
}
```

In the above code, the class Outer has an inner class Inner.
The method callInner() instantiates the Inner class and
invokes its readValue method.

083. What is "method–local" inner class.

Answer:

A method-local inner class is an inner class which is
defined within a method of an enclosing class. It needs to be
instantiated within the method itself and cannot be instantiated
outside the method. It uses only final variables within the
method. It can only have abstract and final modifier.
The following code demonstrates a method local inner class:

```
public class Outer {
  public void doSomething() {
    final int i = 10;
    class Inner{
      void doSomethingInInner() {
        System.out.println(i);
      }
    }
    Inner inner = new Inner();
    inner.doSomethingInInner();
  }
}
```

This code specifies a class Outer with a method

doSomething(). There in a class Inner defined within this
method. Inner is a method local class. It is instantiated within
the method itself.

084. Explain static nested classes with a code sample

Answer:

A static nested class is simply an inner class that has the static
keyword. The following code demonstrates this:

```
public class MyClass {
    int ivalue = 1000; // Line 1
    static int staticValue = 10;
    static class Nested {
        void doSomething() {
            staticValue = 6; //Line 2
            //ivalue = 20; //Line 3
        }
    }
}
```

A static nested class can only access static variables from the
outer class, it cannot access the non–static outer class variables.
So, Line 2 works without any issue, however uncommenting
Line 3 will cause a compilation error.

085. Explain with a code sample how a static nested class can be instantiated

Answer:

Consider the following code snippet:

```
class MyClass {
    int ivalue = 1000; //Line 1
    static class Nested { //Line 2
```

```
    }
}
```

The static nested class can be instantiated as follows:

```
MyClass.Nested nested = new MyClass.Nested();
```

To instantiate a static nested class, both the outer class name and the nested class name need to be specified. In the above code, the class name is `MyClass` and the Static Nested class name is `Nested`.

Inheritance

CHAPTER

08

086. Give an example of illegal method overriding

Answer:

The following code is an example of illegal method overriding::

```
class Electronics {
public void displayPrice() {}
}
class Camera extends Electronics {
public void displayPrice() throws Exception {}
}
```

In this code snippet, the class Camera is a sub–class of the Electronics class. The displayPrice() method is overridden in the Camera class. However, this code will cause a compilation error. This is because the displayPrice() method in Camera class specifies that it throws an Exception.

One of the rules of method overriding is that the overridden method must not throw a new or a broader checked exception.

087. Explain the super keyword

Answer:

The **super** keyword can be used in a sub–class to access the base class instance fields or methods. It can also be used in a sub–class constructor to invoke the base class constructor. Consider the following code snippet:

```
class Electronics {
    protected double price;
    public void displayPrice(){
    //some code here
    }
}
class Camera extends Electronics {
    String cameraName;
    public void setPrice(double price){
        super.price = price; //Line 1
        super.displayPrice(); Line 2
    }
}
```

This code creates a class called `Electronics` which is the base class and a class called `Camera` which is the sub class. Line 1 uses the super keyword to access the price field in the base class `Electronics`. Line 2 uses the super keyword to access the `displayPrice` method in the class `Electronics`

088. The code snippet below has an error. Identity it and state the reason

```
class Electronics {
   public void displayPrice() {}
}
class Camera extends Electronics {
   public void displayname() {}
}
class TestElectronics {
   public static void main(String argument[]) {
       Electronics e = new Camera(); //Line 1
       Camera c = new Electronics(); //Line 2
   }
}
```

Answer:

In this code snippet, the code at Line 1 will compile fine since a sub–class object can be assigned to a variable of a super–class type. However, the code at Line 2 will cause a compilation error. This is because a super class instance cannot be assigned to a variable of the subclass type.

089. Write a code sample that demonstrates how inheritance can help in code reuse

Answer:

Consider the following code:

```
class Electronics {
   public void displayPrice() { //Line 1
      System.out.println("Price is ...");
   }
}
class Camera extends Electronics {
   public void displayBatteryDuration() {
      System.out.println("Battery can withstand up to
      ... hours");
```

```
      }
  }
  public class TestElectronics {
      public static void main(String argument[]) {
          Camera c = new Camera();
          c.displayPrice(); //Line 2
          c.displayBatteryDuration();
      }
  }
```

In the above code, a class called `Electronics` is defined. It
has a sub–class called `Camera`. There is a `displayPrice()`
method (Line 1) defined in the `Electronics` class. Since
`Camera` is a sub–class, the `displayPrice()` method can
be invoked via a `Camera` instance as done at line 2. So, using
inheritance helps reuse code without having to write it again.

090. Write a Java code sample that demonstrates method overriding.

Answer:

Method overriding occurs when a sub–class method has the
same name and type signature as a method in a superclass.
Consider the following code:

```
  public class Electronics {
      public void charge() {
          System.out.println("All Electronics product has to
          be charged");
      }
  }
  public class Camera extends Electronics {
      public void charge() {
          System.out.println("The Camera has to be charged
          periodically");
```

```
    }
}
```

In the above code, `Camera` is a subclass of `Electronics`. Both classes have a method called `charge()` with the same type signature. So, the `charge()` method in the `Camera` class is said to override the `charge()` method in the `Electronics` class.

091. Explain the extends keyword with a code sample

Answer:

The `extends` keyword can be used to specify that a class is a sub–class of another class. It is specified in the sub–class declaration. It should be followed by the name of the super class. The following code demonstrates this:

```
public class Animal {
}
public class Dog extends Animal {
}
```

Here, `Animal` is a base class and `Dog` is a sub–class. The `extends` keyword is used in the `Dog` class to specify that `Dog` is a sub–class of animal.

092. What will be the output of the following code snippet?

```java
public class Shape {
    public Shape() {
        System.out.println("Shape Constructor");
    }
}
public class Circle extends Shape{
    public Circle() {
        System.out.println("Circle constructor");
    }
    public static void main(String args[]) {
        Circle circle = new Circle();
    }
}
```

Answer:

The above code prints the following output:

```
Shape Constructor
Circle constructor
```

This is because a sub–class constructor automatically invokes a base class constructor. Not only that, the call to the base class constructor occurs before the code in the sub–class constructor is executed. So, in this case, when the Circle constructor is invoked, it first invokes the Shape constructor and then executes the code in the Circle constructor.

093. Explain what will be the output of the following code snippet:

```java
public class Animal {
    public static void saySomething() {
        System.out.println("I am an animal");
    }
}
public class Dog extends Animal {
    public static void saySomething() {
        System.out.println("I am a dog");
    }
    public static void main(String args[]) {
        Animal a = new Animal(); //Line 1
        a.saySomething(); //Line 2
        Animal b = new Dog(); //Line 3
        b.saySomething(); //Line 4
        Dog d = new Dog(); //Line 5
        d.saySomething(); //Line 6
    }
}
```

Answer:

This code will print the following output:

```
I am an animal
I am an animal
I am a dog
```

Lines 1 and 2 create an `Animal` object and invoke the
`saySomething` method which prints "I am an Animal".
Line 3 declares an `Animal` variable b but assigns it an object
of type `Dog`. Line 4 invokes the `saySomething` method
using the variable b. Normally, when a superclass variable
is assigned a sub–class object and an overridden method
is invoked, the version from the sub–class gets executed.
However, in this case though both the `Animal` and `Dog`

classes have the `saySomething` method, it is a static method.
Static methods cannot be overridden. So, Line 4 invokes the
`saySomething` method from `Animal` class and prints `I am`
`an Animal`. Lines 5 and 6 create a `Dog` object and invoke the
`saySomething` method which prints `I am a Dog`.

094. What is the output of the following code snippet?

```java
public class Shape {
   public Shape() {
      System.out.println("Shape Constructor");
   }
   public void printShape() {
      System.out.println("I'm a shape!");
   }
}
public class Circle extends Shape{
   public void printShape() {
      System.out.println("I'm a Circle!");
   }
}
public class Triangle extends Shape {
   public void printShape() {
      System.out.println("I'm a Triangle!");
   }
}
public class ShapeDemo {
   public static void main(String[] args) {
      Shape shape = new Shape(); //Line 1
      shape.printShape();

      Shape circle = new Circle(); //Line 2
      circle.printShape();

      Shape triangle = new Triangle(); //Line 3
      triangle.printShape();
   }
}
```

Answer:

This code prints the following output:

```
I'm a shape!
I'm a Circle!
I'm a Triangle!
```

Here, Shape is a base class with Circle and Triangle
sub–classes. There is a printShape method in the base class
that is overridden in both the sub–classes. When a method is
overridden, the type of object assigned and not the reference
variable determines which version of the overridden method
gets invoked. At Line 1, a variable of type Shape is assigned a
Shape object, so the printShape method in the Shape class
is invoked. At Line 2, a variable of type Shape is assigned a
Circle object, so the printShape method in the Circle
class is invoked. At Line 3, a variable of type Shape is assigned
a Triangle object, so the printShape method in the
Triangle class is invoked. This feature of Java is known as
runtime polymorphism.

095. Explain what is the issue with the following code snippet:

```
public class Base {
   public void doSomething() {
   }
}
public class Sub extends Base{
   public void doSomethingElse() {
   }
}
public class Demo {
   public static void main(String[] args) {
      Base base = new Base(); //Line 1
      base.doSomethingElse(); //Line 2
   }
}
```

Answer:

This code causes a compilation error at Line 2. It defines a class called Base and a sub–class called Sub. Line 1 creates a Base class object. Line 2 invokes the base.doSomethingElse() method. Since the doSomethingElse() method is defined in Sub, Base does not have access to it and so a compilation error occurs at Line 2.

096. Why is dynamin method dispatch?

Answer:

Dynamic method dispatch is the mechanism by which the version of an overridden method that will be invoked is determined at run time. Java achieves run time polymorphism via dynamic method dispatch. In Java, a super–class reference variable can be assigned an object of a sub–class. When an overridden method is invoked via a super–class reference object, the version of the method to be invoked is determined based on the type of object that is assigned to the superclass variable. So, if a sub–class object is assigned to a super–class variable and an overridden method is invoked, then the method from the sub–class gets executed. This mechanism allows different methods to be executed using the same method call.

097. Is the following code valid? Explain

```
public class Shape {
}
public class Circle extends Shape{
}
public class ShapeDrawer {
   public void drawShape(Shape shape) {
      System.out.println("Drawing Shape..");
   }
}
public class ShapeDemo {
   public static void main(String args[]) {
      ShapeDrawer shapeDrawer = new ShapeDrawer();
      shapeDrawer.drawShape(new Shape()); //Line 1
      shapeDrawer.drawShape(new Circle()); //Line 2
   }
}
```

Answer:

Yes, the above code is valid. This code defines a base class called `Shape` with a sub–class called `Circle`. There is a `ShapeDrawer` class with a method called `drawShape`. The `drawShape` method accepts as parameter a `Shape` instance. Line 1 invokes the `ShapeDawer.drawShape()` method with a `Shape` object which is valid. Line 2 invokes the `ShapeDawer.drawShape()` method with a `Circle` object. Since `Circle` is a sub–class of `Shape`, it is okay to pass a `Circle` object to the `drawShape` method. In general, you can pass a sub–class object to a method that accepts an object of the super–class type.

098. Why does Java not support multiple inheritance?

Answer:

Multiple inheritance occurs when a class inherits from two classes. Java does not support multiple inheritance as it causes an ambiguity known as the diamond problem. Consider the following code snippet:

```
public class Base1 {
   public void myMethod() {
      System.out.println("Base1.myMethod");
   }
}
public class Base2 {
   public void myMethod() {
      System.out.println("Base2.myMethod");
   }
}
```

This code defines 2 classes called `Base1` and `Base2`. Both have a method called `myMethod`. Now consider the following code snippet:

```
public class Sub extends Base1,Base2{
   }
```

The class `Sub` extends both `Base1` and `Base2`. A sub–class inherits all the members of the base class. Since both have a method called `myMethod`, this results in an ambiguity since it is unclear which method will be inherited by `Sub`. So, Java does not allow this and the above code results in a compilation error.

099. Explain with a code sample how you can prevent a method from being overridden

Answer:

You can prevent a method from being overridden using the final keyword. The final keyword needs to be specified in the method declaration. The following code demonstrates this:

```
public class Base {
    public final void doSomething() {
        System.out.println("Doing something in Base");
    }
}
```

Here, the class Base has a doSomething method that is marked as final. So, it cannot be overridden in the sub–class Suppose we create a sub–class as follows:

```
public class Sub extends Base{
    public void doSomething() { //Line 3
        System.out.println("Doing something in Sub"); //
        Line 4
    } //Line 5
}
```

Here, the sub–class Sub overrides the doSomething method from Base. Since doSomething is final, this will result in a compilation error at Lines 3–5

100. The code below has an error. Identify it and state how it can be fixed.

```
public class Base {
   public void doSomething() { //Line 1
      System.out.println("Doing something in Base");
   }
}
public class Sub extends Base{
   private void doSomething() { //Line 2
      System.out.println("Doing something in Sub");
   }
}
```

Answer:

Here, the base class `Base` has a `doSomething` method that is marked as `public`. The sub–class `Sub` overrides the `doSomething` method. However, it is marked as `private` in the sub–class at Line 2. So, Line 2 causes a compilation error. This is because, you cannot reduce the visibility of an overridden method. In order to fix the error, you need to mark the `doSomething` method at Line 2 as public.

Abstract Classes and Interfaces

101. What are the possible ways of declaring an interface?

Answer:

Following are the possible ways of declaring an interface:

```
a. interface Interface1 {}
b. public interface Interface2 {}
c. public abstract interface Interface3 {}
d. abstract interface Interface4 {}
e. abstract public interface Interface5 {}
```

So, an interface can either have the public access specifier or no specifier which means it will have default access. It can also have the abstract keyword. The order of the keywords does not matter, they can be specified in any order.

102. Explain abstract class with a code sample

Answer:

An abstract class is a class with zero or more abstract methods. An abstract method is a method that has no body. Both the abstract method as well as the class needs to have the abstract keyword specified. The following code demonstrates an abstract class:

```java
public abstract class Animal {
    private String name;
    public abstract void speak() ;
    public void printName(){
        System.out.println(name);
    }
}
```

Here, `Animal` is an abstract class. It has a method called `speak` which is abstract. It also has a concrete method called `printName`

103. Explain with a code sample how to implement an interface

Answer:

In order to implement an interface, you need to use the `implements` keyword after the class name. The implements keyword needs to be followed by the interface name. You also need to provide an implementation for the methods in the interface. The following code demonstrates this:

```java
public interface ShapeDrawer {
    public void draw();
}
```

This code defines an interface called `ShapeDrawer` with a method called `draw`. The following is a class that implements this interface:

```
public class Triangle implements ShapeDrawer{
   public void draw() {
      // code to draw shape
   }
}
```

The class name i.e. `Triangle` is followed by the `implements` keyword which is followed by the name of the interface that is `ShapeDrawer`. Also, the `Triangle` class has code for the `draw` method.

104. Is the following code snippet valid? Explain the reasons either ways

```
public abstract class MyAbstractClass {
   public void doSomething() {
      //doing something
   }
   public static void main(String args[]) {
      MyAbstractClass obj = new MyAbstractClass();//
      Line 1
      obj.doSomething(); //Line 2
   }
}
```

Answer:

The above code is not valid and causes a compilation error at Line 1. This code declares a class called `MyAbstractClass` which is abstract. Line 1 instantiates the class and Line 2 invokes the `doSomething` method. However, you cannot create an object of an abstract class. Although this class does not contain any abstract method, the class is still declared as abstract and so it cannot be instantiated.

105. Can a class implement two interfaces? What will happen if both the interfaces have a method with the same name?

Answer:

Yes, a class can implement two interfaces. Even if both interfaces have a method with the same name, this does not result in an ambiguity as the implementation provided in the class is used.

The following code demonstrates this:

```java
public interface MyInterface1 {
    public void doSomething();
}
public interface MyInterface2 {
    public void doSomething();
}
public class MyClass implements
MyInterface1,MyInterface2{
    @Override
    public void doSomething() {
    // code here
    }
}
MyClass obj = new MyClass();
obj.doSomething(); //Line 1
```

The above code specifies two interfaces MyInterface1, MyInterface2. Both interfaces have a method called doSomething. The code also specifies a class MyClass that implements both the interfaces. It needs to provide an implementation for the doSomething method. When Line 1 is executed, the doSomething() method from MyClass is executed.

106. What is the use of abstract classes?

Answer:

There are often programming situations when you want to create a super–class that is shared by a number of sub–classes. You may want to put some common code in the super class but leave it to the individual classes to provide the specific details. Abstract classes are useful in such scenarios. So, you can create an abstract super–class. You can have concrete methods that implement the common functionality and abstract methods for the functionality that is sub–class specific. The sub–classes can then extend the abstract class and provide implementation for the abstract methods.

107. Explain what is the issue with the following code snippet:

```
public abstract final class MyAbstractClass {
   public void doSomething() {
   }
}
```

Answer:

The above code snippet is not valid. This code declares a class called `MyAbstractClass` that has both the abstract as well as final keyword. An abstract class cannot be final and vice versa. This is because an abstract class needs to have a sub–class that implements the abstract methods in the class. Final is the opposite of abstract, a class marked as final cannot be overridden.

108. Is the following code snippet valid? Explain the reasons either ways

```
public interface ShapeDrawer {
   public void draw();
}
public class Triangle implements ShapeDrawer
   {
   public void draw () {
   // code to draw shape
   }
   public static void main(String args[]) {
      ShapeDrawer shapeDrawer = new Triangle(); //Line
      1
      shapeDrawer.draw(); //Line 2
   }
}
```

Answer:

The above code is valid. This code declares an interface called ShapeDrawer and a class Triangle that implements this interface. Line 1 declares a variable of type ShapeDrawer and assigns it an object of type Triangle. This is valid, you can assign an object of a class that implements an interface to a variable of the interface type. Line 2 then invokes the draw method. This executes the code in the draw method in the Triangle class.

109. Which lines in the following code will cause a compilation error?

```
public interface MyInterface {
   private static int FIELD1 = 7; //Line 1
   int FIELD2 = 8;//Line 2
   public final int FIELD3; //Line 3
   public static int FIELD4 = 8; //Line 4
}
```

Answer:

In the above code, Lines 1 and 3 will cause a compilation error. All the fields declared in an interface need to be public static and final. If the public static and final keywords are not specified, the field is implicitly made `public static final`. Line 1 explicitly specifies the `private` keyword and so causes a compilation error. Line 2 does not have the `public static final` keywords specified. However, this does not cause a compilation error, Java implicitly makes the field `public`, static and final. Line 3 specifies the public and `final` keyword but does not initialize the field. A `final` field needs to be initialized. So, Line 3 causes a compilation error as well. Line 4 specifies the public and static keywords and initializes the field. It does not specify the final keyword. However, this again does not cause a compilation error, the field is implicitly treated as final.

110. Is the code snippet below valid? Explain

```
public abstract class MyAbstractClass {
    private abstract void doSomething();
}
```

Answer:

The above code is invalid and causes a compilation error for the `doSomething` method. This is because the `doSomething ()` method is both `abstract` and `private`. An `abstract` method cannot be made `private`. A `private` method is not accessible in the sub–class. An `abstract` method needs to be accessible in the sub–class in order for the sub–class to provide an implementation for the method. A sub–class will not be able to provide an implementation for an abstract private method.

Packages and Access Control

111. What is a package? What are the advantages of packages?

Answer:

A package is a collection of related Java types. So, a package can include related classes, interfaces and enumerations. Having a package has several advantages as follows:

a. Packages help to keep related code together

b. A package helps avoiding naming collisions. So, you can have a class or some other Java type with the same name in different packages.

c. Packages also help to control access. Code that is outside the package cannot access code within the package unless explicitly allowed via the public keyword.

112. Explain the Java access specifiers.

Answer:

Access specifiers control where a particular member is accessible. They are just some keywords that are specified with class members. They can be specified with an instance field as well as a method. Java has 4 access specifiers as follows:

a. **Private** – A member having the private access specifier is accessible only from within the class in which it is declared.

b. **Protected** – A member having the protected access specifier is accessible to all classes within the package as well as sub-classes that are outside the package

c. **Public** – A member having the public access specifier is accessible to all classes outside the package

d. **Default** – The default access occurs when none of the above access specifiers are specified. In such a case, the member is accessible within the package but not outside the package.

113. Explain with a code sample how to create a package

Answer:

You can create a package by using the `package` keyword. It should be followed by the name that you want to give to the package. The package name should be a valid Java identifier. The package statement should be the first statement in the java file. The following code demonstrates this:

```
package demo;
public class MyClass {
    //instance fields and methods
}
```

This code declares a class called `MyClass`. It is in a package called demo. Note that the package statement is the first statement in the code.

114. Name some default packages in JDK and explain what they do in brief

Answer:

The following are some default packages in Java:

a. `java.util.Collection` – This package includes all the Collection API classes. So, classes/interfaces like List, ArrayList, Set, HashSet, Map, HashMap are all part of this package. In addition, it also has other classes like Date and Calendar for Date handling

b. `java.io` – This package has classes that help to perform input/output operations like InputStream, FileInputStream, FileOutputStream, BufferedReader, BufferedWriter, etc

c. `java.awt` – This package has all classes for creating user interfaces like Component, Container, Frame, etc

d. `java.util.concurrent` – This package has all classes that are useful for concurrent programming like Future, Executor, ExecutorService, etc

115. Is the following code valid? Explain the reasons

```
package demo1;
public class Base {
    protected int a;
}
package demo2;
public class Sub extends Base {
    public void doSomething() {
        System.out.println("Value of a is "+a);
    }
}
```

Answer:

The above code is valid and does not cause any compilation or run time error. This code creates a super class called `Base` and a sub-class called `Sub`. Both classes are in different packages. The Base class has a protected field `a` which is accessed in the sub-class `doSomething()` method. This is perfectly valid. Only `private` fields from the base class are not accessible in the sub-class. Fields with the `protected` access specifier are accessible in the sub-class even if the sub-class is in a different package.

116. Explain the import keyword

Answer:

The `import` keyword is used to include other packages in your code. You can import the standard Java packages like java.util, etc or you can import user defined packages.

The `import` keyword needs to be followed by the package name. In order to import a specific class from a package, you need to specify the class name as well. In order to import the entire package, you need to use a wildcard character (*) after the package name. The following are some examples of import:

```
import.java.util.List; //imports the List interface
import java.io.*; //imports all classes from the java.io
package
```

117. Explain the differences between the protected and default access specifier

Answer:

There are several differences between the protected and default access specifier. These are as follows:

a. The protected access specifier is specified via the protected keyword while the default access occurs when no other access specifier is used. So, the default access specifier does not have a separate keyword

b. When a member has the protected access specifier, that member is accessible to all classes within the package as well as sub–classes that are outside the package too. When a member has the default access specifier, that member is accessible only to classes within the package, it is not accessible outside the package.

118. Is the following code snippet valid? Explain

```
package demo1;
public class MyClass1 {
    int a;   //Line 1
}
package demo2;
public class MyClass2 {
public void doSomething() {
    MyClass1 obj = new MyClass1(); //Line 2
    obj.a = 5; //Line 3
  }
}
```

Answer:

The above code is not valid and will cause a compilation error at line 3. The class `MyClass1` is in a package called `demo1`. It has a field a. Since no access specifier is included explicitly, this field has default access. The class `MyClass2` is in a package called `demo2`. The `doSomething()` method access the field a from `MyClass1` at Line 3. A field with default access is not accessible outside the package so Line 3 will cause a compilation error.

119. Explain what happens when the following code is compiled and executed:

```
package com.questions;
public class CoreJava {
    private String getQuestion() {
        return "Question1";
    }
}
package com.questions;
class JSP extends CoreJava {
    public void getJSPQuestion() {
        Sytem.out.println(getQuestion());
    }
}
```

Answer:

The above code will not compile. The class `CoreJava` defines a private method `getQuestion()`. The `getJSPQuestion()` method in the sub–class invokes this private super–class method. Since a private method cannot be accessed by a sub–class, a compilation error occurs.

120. Explain the java.lang package

Answer:

The `java.lang` package has classes that are important to the Java programming language. It includes the wrapper classes like `Byte`, `Boolean`, `Integer`, `Double`, etc. It has classes like `String`, `StringBuffer` and `StringBuilder` which are useful for String manipulation. It has classes like `Thread`, `Runnable` which are useful for creating multi–threaded applications. It has `Throwable` and other `Exception` classes which are useful for Java's exception handling feature.

Exception Handling

121. Explain 'throw', 'throws' and 'Throwable' in Java.

Answer:

The throws keyword is used to specify that a particular method throws an unhandled exception or multiple exceptions which need to be handled separately. It basically specifies that you do not want to handle the error condition within the method but want to delegate the exception handling to some other part of your code.

The throw keyword is used inside a method to explicitly throw an exception.

Throwable is the base class in the exception hierarchy. Custom exceptions can be created by extending the 'Throwable' class.

122. What will be the output when you compile and execute the following code?

```
class Test {
   try {
      System.out.println("This is try block");
   }

      System.out.println("Try block is executed"); //
      Line 1
   catch(Exception exp) {
      System.out.println("This is catch block");
   }
}
```

Answer:

The above code will not compile and will throw a compilation error. This is because the code at Line 1 is written after the end of try block but before the catch block. All the code needs to be written either inside the try block or the catch block. Java does not allow code in between the try and catch blocks.

123. Write a code sample that demonstrates the try/catch/finally block:

Answer:

Following is code sample that demonstrates the try/catch/finally block:

```
try {
   System.out.println("This is try block");
} catch {
   System.out.println("This is catch block");
}
finally {
   System.out.println("This is finally block");
}
```

All the code that needs to be monitored for exceptions should be placed within the try block. Immediately following the try block, you need to specify a catch clause. In the catch block, you need to specify the exception type that you wish to catch and the code that you want to be executed when that exception occurs. The finally clause is optional and it needs to be placed either after the try or catch block. Any code that needs to be executed always irrespective of whether an exception occurs or not should be placed in the finally clause.

124. What will be the output on executing the code below?

```java
class ExceptionTest {
    public static void main(String argument[]) {
        callMethod();
    }
static void callMethod() {
    int intValue = 100 / 0;
        System.out.println("intValue is: "+intValue);
    }
}
```

Answer:

The above code gets compiled without any errors. However, on executing it throws an `ArithmeticException` with a stack trace (Error information or report) as shown below:

```
Exception in thread "main" java.lang.
ArithmeticException: / by zero
at ExceptionTest.callMethod(ExceptionTest.java:12)
at ExceptionTest.main(ExceptionTest.java:9)
```

This is because dividing a number by 0 is not allowed.

125. Explain the try–catch–finally statement in Java.

Answer:

The Try–Catch–Finally statement allows exception handling in Java. You can put the statements that that you would like to monitor for errors within the try block. The code that needs to be executed in case an exception occurs should be placed within the catch block. You also need to specify the type of exception that you wish to catch. You can specify multiple catch blocks for different types of exceptions. Following the catch block, you can specify the finally block. Here, you need to put in code that you need to be executed irrespective of whether an exception is thrown or not. The catch and finally block are optional, but you need to have either one of them. The following code demonstrates the try–catch–finally statement:

```
try {
    // Code to be monitored for exceptions
}
catch (ExceptionType 1) {
    // Instructions to follow if an exception occurs
}
catch (ExceptionType 2) {
    // Instructions to follow if an exception occurs
}
catch (ExceptionType n) {
    // Instructions to follow if an exception occurs
}
finally {
    // this block is definitely executed even if an
    exception is thrown or not
}
```

126. What will be the output of the following code snippet?

```
public class MyClass1 {
public static void main(String abc[]) {
    try {
        int no;
        no = 52 / 0; //Line 1
    } catch (ArithmeticException e) { //Line 2
        System.out.println("ArithmeticException");
    } catch (ArrayIndexOutOfBoundsException e) { //
    Line 3
        System.out.println("Array Out Of Bound");
    } catch (Exception e) { // any other exception
    //Lin2 4
        System.out.println("Sorry Unhandled
        Exception");
    } finally { // this will be executed //Line 5
        System.out.println("I am done!");
    }
    System.out.println("Thank You!!"); //Line 6
    }
}
}
```

Answer:

This code prints the following output:

```
ArithmeticException
I am done!
Thank You!!
```

Line 1 causes an `ArithmeticException`. This is caught by the `ArithmeticException` catch block at Line 2 which prints the text **ArithmeticException**. Since finally block is always executed, irrespective of whether an error occurs or not, the control then transfers to the finally block at Line 5 and prints **I am done**. Next, control transfers outside the finally block to Line 6 and the code prints **Thank You!!**

127. Suppose you have a method called myMethod with some code that can throw a checked Exception. How will you handle this in the code?

Answer:

If a method throws a checked exception, there are two ways that it can be handled?

a. Use try/catch within the method body as follows:

```
public void myMethod() {
    try {
    //code here
    }
    catch (CheckedException e) {
    }
}
```

Here, when the code throws a **CheckedException**, it is caught by the catch block within the method

b. Use throws clause with the method declaration

```
public void myMethod () throws CheckedException{
    //code here
}
```

Here, when the code throws a **CheckedException**, it is thrown outside the method by the **throws** clause. So, the code that invokes this method needs to handle the exception.

128. What is the use of "finally" clause? Give an example.

Answer:

Any code that needs to be always executed irrespective of whether an exception occurs or not, should be placed within the finally clause. So, for example clean–up code like closing database connections or files on the file system or other resources can be placed in the finally clause. If such code is placed in the try block, there is a possibility that it may not execute if an exception occurs. So, to ensure that such code is always executed, it needs to be placed in the finally block.

129. Explain the differences between Error and Exception

Answer:

The `java.lang.Throwable` is the superclass of all the exception classes. It has two sub–classes, Exception and Error. There are several differences between the two:

a. An Exception represents programmatic errors that are caused by the application itself like accessing a null value, dividing by 0, error while writing to a file, etc. An Error represents errors that occur outside your code within the runtime environment like running out of memory, etc.

b. Exceptions are conditions that an application can handle and recover from. Errors on the other hand are abnormal conditions that indicate serious problems that an application cannot recover from

c. Exceptions are both checked as well as unchecked. Checked exceptions need to be handled or specified within the throws clause in the method declaration. Errors on the other hand are always unchecked and need not be declared in the throws clause

130. What is a RuntimeException?

Answer:

The `java.lang.RuntimeException` is a sub–class of the `java.lang.Exception` class. The `RuntimeException` and its sub–classes are also known as unchecked exceptions.

This is because the compiler does not force you to handle such exceptions. So even if code that might potentially throw an unchecked exception is written, the compiler does not cause an error. Some examples of `RuntimeExceptions` are `ArithmeticException`, `NullPointerException`, `ArrayIndexOutOfBoundsException`.

String Handling

CHAPTER 12

131. What is a string literal? Give an example..

Answer:

A string literal is a set of characters enclosed in double quotes. It can be assigned to a String variable with the help of the assignment operator (=). The following line of code shows that the string literal "I'm a literal" is assigned to the string variable called 'name'.

```
String name = "I'm a literal";
```

132. What will be the output of the following code? Explain why

```
class StringDemo {
   public static void main (String strArgs[]) {
      String strVar = "Welcome";
      strVar.concat(" to Java");
      System.out.println(strVar);

   }
}
```

Answer:

This code prints the following output:

```
Welcome
```

Java strings are immutable objects so unless explicitly assigned, the string's value does not change. The method `concat ()` simply appends the value **to Java** to `strVar` but does not assign the appended String back to the variable `strVar`.

In order for the String `Welcome to Java` to be printed, the code needs to be modified as follows:

```
strVar = strVar.concat(" to Java");
```

133. What will be the output when the following code is executed?

```
StringBuffer stringBuffer = new StringBuffer();
stringBuffer.append("Core ");
stringBuffer.append("Java");
System.out.println("The resultant StringBuffer Value
is: "+stringBuffer);
```

Answer:

On executing the code above, it will print the following output:

```
The resultant StringBuffer Value is: Core Java
```

The `StringBuffer.append()` method appends the specified

value to the value in the StringBuffer

134. What will be the output of the following code snippet?

```
String xValue = "xyz";
String yValue = xValue.concat("qrs").toUpperCase().
replace('Z', 'c');
System.out.println(yValue);
```

Answer:

The code above prints the following output:

```
XYcQRS
```

First, xValue is concatenated with the value **qrs** and so
the value becomes **xyzqrs**. Then, the value is converted to
uppercase and so, the value becomes **XYZQRS**. Then, the
character **Z** is replaced with **c** and so, the value becomes
ZYcQRS.

135. What are the various ways of assigning a string literal to a String variable?

Answer:

Following are the various ways of assigning a string literal to a
string variable:

```
a. String strValue1 = "String Literal 1";

b. String strValue2 = new String("String
   Literal 2");

c. String strValue3 = new String();
   strValue3 = "String Literal 3";

d. String strValue4 = strValue3;
```

Approach **a** creates the String variable strValue1 by assigning a String literal to it. Approach **b** creates the variable strValue2 by using the String constructor that accepts a String value. Approach **c** creates the variable strValue3 using the default String constructor and later assigns a value to it. Approach **d** creates the variable strValue4 by assigning another String variable to it.

136. Name some commonly used methods from the String class

Answer:

The following are some commonly used methods from the String class:

a. **concat()** – This is used to append a value to the current String.

b. **length()** – This is used to find the length of the String, that is the total number of characters in the String.

c. **replace()** – This is used to replace a particular character or characters from a String with some other value

d. **substring()** – This is used to obtain a substring of the current string that begins from the specified position

e. **trim()** – This is used to remove the whitespaces in a string

f. **toUpperCase()** – This is used to convert all the characters in a string to upper case

g. **toLowerCase()** – This is used to convert all the characters in a string to lower case

h. **equals()** – This is used to compare the current String with the specified String. It returns a boolean value which is the result of comparison.

i. **equalsIgnoreCase()** – This is used to compare the current String with the specified String irrespective of the case. It returns a boolean value which is the result of comparison.

137. What is the difference between StringBuffer and StringBuilder?

Answer:

Both StringBuffer and StringBuilder classes can be used to perform String operations. They are both mutable unlike the java.lang.String which is immutable. However, the StringBuilder class is not thread safe i.e., StringBuilder methods are not synchronized. That means, StringBuilder should not be used when you execute two or more threads in an application. Also, since StringBuilder it unsynchronized, it has a better performance as compared to StringBuffer.

138. Write a code sample that reverses a String without using a loop.

Answer:

There are several ways that you can reverse a String without using a loop. One of the ways is to use the reverse method on the StringBuilder class. The following code demonstrates this:

```
StringBuilder sBuilder = new StringBuilder("Core Java");
sBuilder.reverse();
System.out.println(sBuilder);
```

This code creates a StringBuilder instance with the String **Core Java** and then invokes the reverse() method on it.

So, this code prints the following output:

```
avaJ eroC
```

The StringBuffer class also has a method called reverse() which can be used to reverse a String.

139. Write a code sample that demonstrates how you can convert a String to uppercase.

Answer:

The String class has a method called `toUpperCase()`. This can be used to convert a String to uppercase. The following code demonstrates this:

```
String myStr = "Hello World";
myStr = myStr.toUpperCase();
System.out.println(myStr);
```

This code creates a String called `myStr` with the value `Hello World`. It invokes the `toUpperCase()` method on this String object. So, this code prints the following output:

```
HELLO WORLD
```

140. Explain how you can convert an Integer to a String

Answer:

There are several ways in which you can convert an Integer to a String. These are as follows:

a. Directly enclosing the Integer in quotes – You can enclose the number in quotes and assign to a String variable as follows:

```
String strNum = "10";
```

b. Using `String.valueOf` – The String class has a `valueOf` method. You can use this to convert an Integer to a String as shown below:

```
String strNum = String.valueOf(10);
```

c. Using the `Integer.toString` method – The Integer class has a `toString` method. This can also be used to convert an Integer to String as shown below:

```
String numStr2 = new Integer(10).toString();
```

Generics

CHAPTER 13

141. What happens when you compile and run the following code?

```
class Mammal {}
class Cat extends Mammal { }
List<Mammal> list = new ArrayList<Cat>();
```

Answer:

This code will not compile. This is because Mammal is specified for List while Cat is specified for ArrayList. The rule is that the type of the variable declaration must match the type that you specify for the implementation. So, the same data type needs to be specified in the List and ArrayList.

142. Will Line 1 in the following line of code compile? If not, state the reasons.

```
class Mammal {}
class Cat extends Mammal { }
List<? super Mammal> mList = new ArrayList<Cat>(); //
line 1
```

Answer:

Line 1 will cause a compilation error. This is because `Cat` is at a lower level of hierarchy than `Mammal`. `Mammal` is the super class. So, the above code will compile only if `<Cat>` is replaced with `<Mammal>` or `<Object>`.

143. Explain the issue with the following code.

```
List<?> mylist = new ArrayList<? extends Mammal>();
```

Answer:

The above line of code creates a List named `mylist`. It specifies the wild card notation (? Symbol) in the List declaration. This is incorrect and causes a compilation error because a wildcard notation cannot be used in the declaration part. Wildcard notations for generics are only allowed only in method parameters or return values.

144. Explain what additional code is required to make the code snippet below valid:

```
public void getList(T t)
```

Answer:

This code declares a method called `getList()` with a generic argument. In order for this code to be valid, this method must be inside a class that accepts a generic type as follows:

```
public class MyClass<T> {
   public void getList(T t){

   }
}
```

145. Explain Bounded Generic Types with a code sample

Answer:

Bounded Generic Types help to restrict the type that can be used as a generic argument. The following code demonstrates this:

```
public class Shape {
}
public class Circle extends Shape{
}
public class ShapeDrawer<T extends Shape> {
   public void drawShape(T shape) {
      System.out.println("Drawing Shape..");

   }
}
```

This code declares a superclass called Shape that has a sub-class called Circle. It also specifies a class called ShapeDrawer which is a generic type. Instead of directly specifying T, the code specifies T extends Shape. This means that the generic type T should be a sub-class of Shape. So, if the drawShape method is invoked with an argument which is not a sub-class of Shape, a compilation error will occur.

Collections

146. What are the four main interfaces in the Java Collection API

Answer:

java.util.Collection is the top level interface in the Java Collection API. It simply represents a group of values operated as one unit. It has two main sub–interfaces Set and List. Both are used to store a group of values; however, they differ slightly in the way they store data.

A List allows duplicate elements i.e. the same element can be present more than once. Also, a List is ordered i.e. elements in a list are stored in the order in which they are inserted & this order is maintained.

A Set does not allow duplicates & is unordered so the order in which the elements are inserted into the Set will not be maintained.

There is another top–level interface called Map. A Map is used to store key–value pairs.

147. How will you search for a specific element in an array?

Answer:

Java provides the `java.util.Arrays` class as part of the Collection framework. This has several utility methods. Once such method is the `Arrays.binarySearch` method which can be used to search for a specific element in an array. It returns an integer which specifies the position of the element being searched if present. Otherwise, it returns –1.

The following code demonstrates the `binarySearch()` method:

```
String [] strArr = {"one", "two", "four"};
System.out.println("Search index of one is:
"+Arrays.binarySearch(strArr, "one"));
```

This code prints the following output:

```
Search index of one is:0
```

Since the String one is at position **0**, so the `binarySearch()` method returns **0**

148. Which collection would you choose if do not want duplicates and do not care about the order?

Answer:

HashSet should be used if you want to avoid duplicates and do not care about the order. HashSet is an implementation of the Set interface. It is unsorted and unordered. In addition, TreeSet and LinkedHashSet are also Set implementations. Both of these do not allow duplicates. However, TreeSet maintains the sorting order while LinkedHashSet maintains the insertion order.

149. Explain with a code sample how you can remove the head of a queue

Answer:

The interface Queue has a method called `poll()` which is used to remove the head of the queue.

The following code demonstrates this:

```
Queue<Integer> lList = new LinkedList<Integer>();
lList.add(100);
lList.add(200);
System.out.println("Removed: "+lList.poll()); // Line 1
```

This code creates a Queue and adds two integer values to it. It then invokes the `poll()` method. So, this code prints the following output:

```
The Element removed is: 100
```

So, the `poll()` method always removes the head of the queue i.e., the first element added in the queue.

150. Which collection implementation allows growing or shrinking its size and provides indexed access to its elements?

Answer:

ArrayList is an implementation of the List interface. It allows growing or shrinking its size. It has add/remove methods that increase or decrease the size of the List. It also provides indexed access to its elements. It has a get method to achieve this.

The following code demonstrates an ArrayList:

```
List<Integer> myList = new ArrayList<Integer>();
myList.add(2);
myList.add(4);
myList.add(6);
myList.remove(1);
Integer num = myList.get(0);
```

151. Explain the Queue interface.

Answer:

The Queue interface is part of the Collection API and extends the java.util.Collection interface. In addition to Collection operations, Queue provide features of a queue data structure like FIFO (First in First Out). The Queue interface has several methods that allow queue operations:

peek() – allows inspecting the element at the top of the queue

poll() – removes the element at the top of the queue

offer() – insert an element into the queue

152. Explain the Comparator interface

Answer:

Comparator is an interface that can be used for sorting. It has been designated as a functional interface since Java 8. It has a single abstract method called compare. The compare method accepts two objects and returns a boolean value that is the result of comparison. Comparator can also be used to sort custom object. For this, the corresponding class needs to implement the Comparator interface and provide an implementation for the compare method. If you are using Java

8 or a higher version, you can also implement a Comparator using a lambda expression

153. Explain some of the methods on the Queue Interface

Answer:

The following are some of the methods on the Queue Interface:

a. **offer(E e)** – This adds an object to the queue. It does not throw an Exception if it is not possible to add the object to the queue.

b. **peek()** – This returns the last added object in the queue

c. **poll()** – This returns the last added object in the queue and removed it from the queue

d. **remove(Object O)** – This removes the object from the queue

e. **add(E e)** – This adds an object to the queue. This method throws an Exception if it is not possible to add the object to the queue.

154. Is it possible to mix generic and non–generic collections? If so, give example.

Answer:

Yes, it is possible to mix generic and non–generic collections. The following code snippet demonstrates this:

```
public  void insertDouble() {
    List<Double> myDoubleList = new ArrayList<Double>();
    myDoubleList.add(2.0); // Line 1
    myDoubleList.add(4.0); // Line 2
    insertSomethingElse(myDoubleList);
}
public  void insertSomethingElse(List myDoubleList) {//
Line 3
    myDoubleList.add("Hello World"); //Line 4
}
```

In the above code, Line 1 and Line 2 add double literals to the list which is a List with generic Double specified. The code then invoked the `insertSomethingElse()` method with this double List. In the method declaration at Line 3, the generic type is not specified for the `myDoubleList` variable. So, any type of value can be added to this List. Line 4 adds a string literal into the List.

155. What are some of the important methods on the Collection interface?

Answer:

The following are some of the important methods on the Collection interface:

a. **add** – Allows adding an object to the collection

b. **remove** – Allows removing an object from the collection

c. **contains** – Allows checking if an object is present in the collection

d. **size** – Returns the length of the collection

e. **iterate** – Allows iterating over the collection

Enumerations, Autoboxing and Wrapper Classes

CHAPTER

15

156. What are the wrapper classes available in Java?

Answer:

Wrapper classes are classes that corresponding to the Java primitive types. They help to convert primitive types to objects and vice versa. This is particularly useful when you want to use Collections. Since a Collection does not accept primitive values, you can use the corresponding wrapper type. Most of the wrapper classes take their primitive type or String as an argument.

Java supports the following wrapper classes:

Primitive Type	Wrapper Type
byte	Byte
short	Short

int	Integer
long	Long
float	Float
double	Double
char	Character
boolean	Boolean

157. What will be the output of the following code?

```java
public class BooleanDemo {
    public static void main(String a[]){
        //create Boolean using boolean primitive type
        boolean bool = true;
        Boolean booObj1 = new Boolean (bool); //line 1
        System.out.println("Wrapper class Boolean
        output: "+booObj1);
        Boolean booObj2 = new Boolean ("false"); //line
        2
        System.out.println("Wrapper class Boolean
        output: "+booObj2);
        System.out.println(booObj1.booleanValue());
    }
}
```

Answer:

Line 1 creates a boolean wrapper type `boolObj1` corresponding to the `bool` variable. Line 2 creates a boolean wrapper `boolObj2` using a String value. Java automatically converts wrapper types to primitive types. In addition, there is a method called `booleanValue()` on the Boolean wrapper class that returns the primitive boolean value. So, this code will print the following output:

```
Wrapper class Boolean output: true
Wrapper class Boolean output: false
true
```

158. Explain how you will convert a String "100.55" to a Double and a Double 100.55 to a String

Answer:

A String can be converted to a Double using the `Double.parseDouble()` method as shown below:

```
Double doubleValue = Double.parseDouble("100.55");
```

A Double can be converted to a String using the `Double.toString()` method as shown below:

```
String stringValue = Double.toString(100.55);
```

159. What will be the output the following code?

```
Double doubleValue = Double.parseDouble("Java");
System.out.println(doubleValue);
```

Answer:

The above code compiles fine. However, on execution it throws a `NumberFormatException`. This is because the JVM cannot convert the String Java to a Double value.

160. What is a Wrapper class in Java? What are the special properties of Wrapper class objects?

Answer:

Java is an Object–oriented language. The primitive data types in Java are not objects. Sometimes, you will need object equivalents of the primitive types. A good example is when you want to use Collections. Collections can only contain objects and not primitive types. To solve this issue, Java introduced wrapper classes that wrap primitive types into objects. Each primitive has a corresponding wrapper class and you can create an object of that type. In the same way you can convert a wrapper object to the primitive type too. For example, corresponding to the "int" primitive type, Java has the java.lang.Integer wrapper class. Java automatically converts between the primitive types and the corresponding wrapper classes.

161. Explain Autoboxing with an example

Answer:

Autoboxing referred as Boxing or Unboxing is a feature introduced in Java 5 which helps programmers to reduce some lines of code.

For example, in order to assign a primitive value to a wrapper class, you will need to write wrapping code as follows:

```
Integer integerValue = new Integer(1000); //wrapping
```

With autoboxing, the above code can be re-written as follows:

```
Integer integerValue = 1000;
```

So also, in order to assign a wrapper class to a primitive you will need to write unwrapping code as follows:

```
Integer integerValue = 1000;
int iValue = integerValue.intValue(); //unwrapping
```

With autoboxing, the above code can be re-written as follows:

```
Integer integerValue = 1000;
int iValue = integerValue;
```

Threads

CHAPTER 16

162. How will you create Threads in Java?

Answer:

There are two ways in which a Thread can be created in Java:

a. By extending Thread class – In this approach, you need to create a class that extends the in–built Thread class and you need to override the `run()` method. The following code demonstrates this:

```
public class MyThread extends Thread {
    public void run(){
    System.out.println("In Thread Body..");
  }
}
```

b. By implementing the interface called Runnable – In this approach, you need to create a class that implements the in–built Runnable interface. The Runnable interface has a single method called `run()` which you need to implement. The following code demonstrates this:

```
public class MyThread implements Runnable{
    public void run(){
    System.out.println("In Thread Body..");
  }
}
```

163. Explain the different types of Threads in Java

Answer:

There are 2 types of threads –User defined Threads and Daemon threads

User defined threads are those that are created programmatically by a user. These are high priority threads. The JVM waits for these threads to finish.

Daemon threads are mostly created by the JVM, although a user–defined thread can be explicitly set to be a daemon thread as well. Daemon threads are usually used for background processes such as Garbage Collection. As soon as all Non–Daemon threads stop running, the JVM stops running and does not wait for the Daemon threads to stop.

164. Can the run method be invoked directly without invoking the start method?

Answer:

The `run()` method can directly be invoked instead of invoking the `start()` method. However, this will not spawn a new thread, the code within the `run()` method will be executed in the same thread that invokes it. The `start()` method is responsible for spawning a new thread and needs to be invoked.

165. **What happens behind the scenes when the following code is executed?**

```
class Test {
    public static void main(String argument[]) {
        System.out.println("Thread Example...");
    }
}
```

Answer:

When the above code is executed, the JVM creates a thread to run this code. This thread executes the code in the main method after which the program terminates.

166. **Explain some of the main methods in the Thread class**

Answer:

a. **start()** – Initiates the thread and invoke the run() method

b. **run()** – Code that needs to be executed in a separate thread needs to be placed in the run method

c. **sleep()** – makes the running thread pause for the specified time

d. **setName()** – sets the name of the thread to the value specified

e. **join()** – waits for the thread to die for at most the specified time

f. **isAlive()** – Returns a boolean value that indicates if the current thread is alive or not

g. **setPriority()** – Changes the priority of the thread to the specified value.

167. Explain thread states

Answer:

Thread exists in five states. They are as follows:

a. **New** – A thread is in new state when a new Thread is created but the start method is not invoked

b. **Runnable** – A Thread is in the Runnable state after the start() method is invoked but the Thread scheduler has not yet started executing the thread.

c. **Running** – When the thread scheduler starts executing the thread, it is in the Running state. The code within the body of the run() method gets executed

d. **Waiting / Blocking** – If a thread is alive, but not eligible to run, it is said to be in the blocking state.

e. **Dead** – When the thread completes its execution, it enters the dead state

168. Write a code sample that creates a thread using the "Thread" class.

Answer:

The following code creates a thread using "Thread" class:

```
class MyThread extends Thread {
  public static void main(String argument[]) {
    MyThread thread = new MyThread ();
    thread.start(); // Line 1
  }
  public void run() {
    System.out.println("Inside Run Method..");// Line
    2
  }
}
```

The code above defines a class called MyThread that extends the Thread class. When Line 1 is executed, a new thread is spawned. This executes the code specified within the run() method.

169. Write a code sample that creates a thread using the Runnable interface.

Answer:

The following code creates a thread by implementing the "Runnable" interface:

```
class MyThread implements Runnable {
public static void main(String argument[]) {
  MyThread myThread = new MyThread();
  Thread thread = new Thread(myThread); //Line 1
  thread.start(); // Line 2
}
public void run() {
  System.out.println("Inside Run Method..");
  }
}
```

The code above defines a class called MyThread that implements the Runnable interface. A new Thread object is created and the `Runnable` implementation that is `MyThread` instance is passed to it at line 1. When Line 2 is executed, a new thread is spawned. This executes the code specified within the `run()` method.

170. Is it possible to create more than one thread in a Java application? If so, how will the threads communicate with each other?

Answer:

Yes, it is possible to create more than one thread in a Java application. For two threads to communicate with each other, the methods `wait()`, `notify()` and `notifyAll()` from the object class need to be used.

The `wait()` method causes the current thread to pause until some other thread invokes notify on the same object.

If there are many objects that are waiting on a particular object, the `notify()` method causes any one thread to resume.

The `notifyAll()` method causes all the threads that are waiting on a particular object to resume.

171. What is Synchronization?

Answer:

When multiple threads try to access a shared resource at the same time, then they need some way for the resource to be accessed by only one Thread at a time. The process which helps to achieve this is called as synchronization. Java provides a keyword called **synchronized** which helps to achieve this.

172. Explain what happens when the following code is executed

```
class TestMyRunnable implements Runnable {
public void run() {
   System.out.println("Inside Run Method..");
   System.out.println("Name of thread is: "+Thread.
   currentThread().getName());
}
}
class TestMyThread {
public static void main(String argument[]) {
   TestMyRunnable runnable = new TestMyRunnable();
   Thread thread = new Thread(runnable);
   Thread.setName("My Thread"); //Line 1
   thread.start(); //Line 2
}
}
```

Answer:

The code compiles fine and displays the following output:

```
Inside Run Method.
Name of thread is: My Thread
```

When Line 1 is executed, it sets the name of the thread to **My Thread**. So, when Line 2 is executed, it spawns a new thread and executes the code within the run() method which prints the name of the thread as **My Thread**

173. Consider the following code:

```
class TestMyRunnable implements Runnable {
public void run() {
   for (int iValue = 0; iValue < 1000; iValue++)
      System.out.println("Name of thread is: "+Thread.
      currentThread().getName());
   }
   public static void main (String argument[]) {
      TestMyRunnable runnable = new TestMyRunnable();
      Thread threadC = new Thread(runnable);
      Thread threadD = new Thread(runnable);
      threadC.setName("Thread 1");
      threadD.setName("Thread 2");
      threadC.start();
      threadD.start();
   }
}
```

Executing this code first prints "Thread 1" 1000 times and then prints the "Thread 2" 1000 times. If this is incorrect, explain the reasons.

Answer:

On executing the above code, it will not print **Thread 1** 1000 times and then **Thread 2** 1000 times. The order in which the threads execute is up to the Thread scheduler. So though both threads print their names 1000 times, the order in which they print it is not known.

---

174. Write a code sample that makes a thread pause for ten minutes

Answer:

In order to make a thread pause for ten minutes, you need to invoke the sleep() method within the run() method. The sleep() method accepts as parameter a long value which accepts the time that the thread should sleep in milliseconds. The following code demonstrates this:

```
try {
    Thread.sleep(10 * 60 * 1000)
}
catch(InterruptedException exp) {
}
```

175. What happens when a synchronized method is invoked?

Answer:

Whenever a synchronized method is executed, the thread that invokes the method acquires a lock and holds the lock under the end of the method. Only after the current thread completes executing the method it releases the lock. So other threads can then acquire the lock and execute the method. Thus, the synchronized keyword prevents multiple threads from simultaneously executing the code within the synchronized method.

Java IO API

176. What happens when the following code is executed?

```
File myFile = new File("CoreJava.txt");
```

Answer:

When the code above is executed, the JVM creates a Java object called myFile in the memory but the actual file will not be created on the file system. In order to actually create the file, the myFile.createNewFile() method needs to be invoked.

177. Write a code sample that creates a file in the path /usr/test. txt.

Answer:

The following code will create a file test.txt within the /usr/ directory:

```
try {
File txtFile = new File("/usr/test.txt"); // Line 1
txtFile.createNewFile(); // Line 2
} catch (IOException exp) {
}
```

In the above code, when Line 1 is executed, an object `txtFile` is created in memory and when Line 2 is executed, the file **test. txt** is created inside the folder **/usr/**.

178. Explain the FileWriter class with a code sample

Answer:

FileWriter class is used to write characters or Strings to a file without having to convert them to a byte array.

They are usually wrapped within PrintWriter or BufferedWriter which provides performance improvement and more methods for writing data.

The following code demonstrates a FileWriter:

```
try {
    File txtFile = new File("/usr/CoreJava.txt");
    FileWriter myFileWriter = new FileWriter(txtFile);
    myFileWriter.write("Line 1 \n Line 2 \n"); // Line 1
    myFileWriter.flush();
    myFileWriter.close();
} catch (IOException exp) {
}
```

In the above code, when Line 1 is executed, the `write()` method writes the content into the file **CoreJava.txt**.

179. Write a code snippet that reads the content in the file /usr/ CoreJava.txt using a FileReader and displays the output in

the console.

Answer:

The following code demonstrates reading the content in the specified file using a `FileReader` and displaying the output on the console:

```
try {
    File txtFile = new File("F:/CoreJava.txt");
    char [] totalChar = new char[1000];
    FileReader myFileReader = new FileReader(txtFile);
    myFileReader.read(totalChar); //Line 1
    for(char readChar : totalChar) {//Line 2
    System.out.print(readChar);
    }
    myFileReader.close();
 }
    catch (IOException exp) {
}
```

When Line 1 is executed, the `read()` method reads the content from the file and into the `totalChar` array. The for loop at line 2 then prints the contents of the array to the console

180. **Explain with a code sample how you can create a directory on the file system.**

Answer:

There is a method called mkdir() on the File class that creates a directory corresponding to the specified file object. The following code uses this method to create a directory in the file system:

```
File myDirectory = new File("/usr/mydir"); //1
myDirectory.mkdir(); //2
```

Line 1 creates a file object. Line 2 invokes the `mkdir()` method to creates an actual directory.

181. Explain what happens when the following code is compiled and executed

```
File myDirectory = new File("/usr/JavaCodes");
File myNewFile = new File("/usr/JavaCodes/CoreJava.
txt"); //line 1
myNewFile.createNewFile();
```

Answer:

The above code throws an IOException. This is because the directory /usr/JavaCodes/ is not created, only a file object myDirectory corresponding to it is created. In order for the code to work, you need to add the following line of code before Line 1:

```
myDirectory.mkdir();
```

182. Write a code sample that demonstrates the PrintWriter class.

Answer:

The `PrintWriter` is a specialization of the Writer class can be used to write formatted representations of objects. The following code demonstrates how the `PrintWriter` can be used to write a String:

```
File myNewFile = new File("/usr/CoreJava.txt");
PrintWriter myPrintWriter = new PrintWriter(myNewFile);
//Line 1
myPrintWriter.println("This gets inserted into the
File"); //Line 2
   myPrintWriter.close(); //Line 3
```

In the above code, when Line 1 is executed, the file **CoreJava.txt** is created inside the folder **/usr/**.

When Line 2 is executed, the `println()` method writes the String specified in the file **CoreJava.txt** and terminates the line. When Line 3 is executed, the file is closed and the contents are saved in the file.

183. Write a code sample that demonstrates how to delete a file

Answer:

The file class has a method called `delete()` that can be used to delete a file. The following code demonstrates this:

```
File myNewFile = new File("/usr/CoreJava.txt");
boolean success = myNewFile.delete(); //Line 1
```

In the above code, when Line 1 is executed, the `delete()` method deletes the specified file. It returns a boolean value that indicates whether file deletion is successful or not.

184. Write a code sample that demonstrates how to rename a file or directory.

Answer:

The file class has a method called renameTo() which can be used to rename a file or a directory.

The following code demonstrates renaming a file:

```
File file1 = new File("/usr/file1.txt");
file1.createNewFile();
File file2 = new File("/usr/file2.txt");
file1.renameTo(file2); //Line 1
```

This code renames the file "file1.txt" to "file2.txt"

The following code demonstrates renaming a directory:

```
File dir1 = new File("/usr/dir1");
dir1.createNewFile();
File dir2 = new File("/usr/dir2");
dir1.renameTo(dir2); //Line 1
```

This code renames the directory **dir1** to **dir2**

185. Which classes are used to serialize and de–serialize objects?

Answer:

Serialization is the process of writing an object onto the file system. The `java.io. ObjectOutputStream` can be used to serialize objects. It has a `writeObject()` method which can be used to achieve this. De–serialization is the process of restoring a serialized object. The `java.io. ObjectInputStream` can be used to serialize objects. It has a `readObject()` method which can be used to achieve this.

186. Explain some of the important methods on the File class

Answer:

A File class encapsulates a file or directory on the file system. Some of the methods on the file class are as follows:

a. **createNewFile()** – Creates a new empty file

b. **list()** – Returns an array of the files/directories within the current directory

c. **delete** – Deletes the file from the files system

d. **mkdir** – Creates a directory

e. **getAbsolutePath** – Returns the absolute path of the file

Miscellaneous

187. Explain what happens when the following code snippet is compiled

```
public class Test {
public static void main(String argument[]) {
   int iValue;
   System.out.println(iValue);
}
}
```

Answer:

This code will cause a compilation error. This is because the variable iValue is not initialized but used in the Sysout statement. The error can be fixed by initializing the variable iValue before it is used as follows:

```
int iValue = 0;
System.out.println(iValue);
```

188. Explain what happens when the following code is compiled and executed

```
class Calculate {
    float fValue = 10.2f;
    public static void main(String argument[]) {
        System.out.println("Float value is: "+fValue);
    }
}
```

Answer:

The above code will cause a compilation error because the main method tries to access the non–static instance variable fvalue. Java does not allow accessing a static variable from a non–static method.

189. Explain symmetric equals() contract.

Answer:

Suppose that there are two objects v1 and v2. If v1.equals(v2) returns true then v2.equals(v1) must return true. This equals() contract is called as symmetric contract.

Consider the following code:

```
Object v1; Object v2;
v1.equals(v2); //Line 1
v2.equals(v1); //Line 2
```

So, in case of a symmetric contract, Line 1 returns true if and only if Line 2 returns true.

190. Which of the following are invalid statements and why?

```
System.out.println(2+2); //line 1
int i= 2+'2'; //line 2
String s= "one"+'two'; //line 3
byte b=256; //line 4
```

Answer:

Line 1 and line 2 are valid statements.

Line 3 is invalid. The value **two** is not valid since single quotes cannot be used for a String, they can only be used for a character constant. Strings need to be enclosed in double quotes.

Line 4 is invalid. The byte variable **b** cannot be assigned the value 256 since it is out of the range of a byte.

191. What is the use of transient keyword?

Answer:

The transient keyword can be specified on an instance variable. Specifying transient for an instance variable indicates that its state should not be saved when the object is serialized. Consider the following code snippet:

```
class Electronics implements Serializable {
transient private int price; //Line 1
private int quantity; //Line 2
}
```

When an instance of the Electronics class is serialized, the price field will not be serialized, only the quantity field will be serialized

192. What is Garbage Collection in Java?

Answer:

Garbage collection is the process of freeing memory allocated to objects that are no longer used. During runtime, when an object is created, the JVM allocates some memory to hold the object. The JVM periodically checks for objects that are in use and de–allocates the memory for those objects which are not in use anymore. Garbage collection is this process of removing objects that are no longer in use. So, the programmer does not have to bother about manual de–allocation of memory.

193. Which part of the memory is used in Garbage Collection? Which algorithm does the JVM use for Garbage collection?

Answer:

Garbage Collection is done in the heap memory. The JVM uses the mark and swap algorithm internally for garbage collection.

194. When does garbage collection occur?

Answer:

The JVM (Java Virtual Machine) controls the garbage collection process. So, the JVM decides when the garbage collection process should run.

It is also possible to explicitly request garbage collection through Java code via the `System.gc()` or `Runtime.getRuntime().gc()` method. However, there is no guarantee that invoking these methods will run the garbage collector.

195. What code needs to be written in order to trigger garbage collection?

Answer:

Garbage collection can be triggered in one of the following ways:

Method 1: Using `Runtime.gc()` as follows:

```
Runtime runTime = Runtime.getRuntime();
runTime.gc();
```

Method 2: Using `System.gc()` as follows:

```
System.gc();
```

Both these approaches do not guarantee garbage collection, it is up–to the JVM to actually decide when to run the garbage collector

196. **Explain with a code sample how an object becomes eligible for garbage collection.**

Answer:

An object becomes eligible for garbage collection when it is no longer referenced. The following scenarios demonstrate this:

Scenario 1 – Setting the object to null

```
String stringValue = "This is a String value"; //Line 1
stringValue = null; //Makes stringValue
eligible for GC
```

Scenario 2 – Re–assigning a variable

```
String str1 = "Hello";
String str2 = str1; //makes str1 eligible for GC
```

Scenario 3 – Objects created within a method:

```
public void doSomething(){
String str1 = "Hello";
}
public void callMethod(){
doSomething();
//str1 from doSomething becomes eligible for GC
}
```

Functional Interfaces

01

197. What is a functional interface? How can you create a functional interface?

Answer:

A functional interface is an interface that has only one abstract method. In order to create a functional interface, you simply need to create an interface that has just one abstract method as shown below:

```
@FunctionalInterface
public interface Multiplier {
    public int multiply(int a, int b);
}
```

This code defines an interface called Multiplier. It has only a multiply method. It has the @FunctionalInterface annotation specified. This annotation is optional, it marks the interface as a functional interface. So, if you try to add another abstract method to the interface, the code causes a compilation error

198. Explain the java.util.Function package

Answer:

The java.util.function is a new package added by Java 8. It has a lot of built–in functional interfaces. Some of the interfaces in this package are as follows:

a. **Predicate** – This can be used to test a condition. It returns a boolean value which indicates whether the condition is true or false. It accepts an argument of any data type.

b. **Consumer** – This can be used to operate on a value. It accepts an argument of any data type and operates on it. It returns a void

c. **Function** – This can be used to transform an input value. It accepts an argument of any data type, transforms it and returns a result.

d. **Supplier** – This can be used to produce a value. It does not accept any argument, but produces a result of any data type

199. Explain the java.util.function.Consumer interface with a code sample

Answer:

The java.util.function.Consumer is an built–in functional interface. It is part of the `java.util.function` package which is added by Java 8. It has a method called `accept()` that accepts an argument of any data type and operates on it. It does not return any result. This method needs to be implemented via a lambda expression. The following code demonstrates this:

```
Consumer<String> printStr = val -> System.out.
println(val); //Line 1
printStr.accept("Hello World"); //Line 2
```

Line 1 creates a Consumer called `printStr` of String type. It implements the `accept()` method via a lambda expression that simply prints the input String. Line 2 invokes the `accept` method with the value "`Hello World`". So, this code prints the following output:

```
Hello World
```

200. Explain the differences between the Supplier and Consumer interfaces.

Answer:

Both the Supplier and Consumer interfaces are built–in functional interfaces in the `java.util.function` package. There are several differences between the two as follows:

a. The Supplier interface does not accept an argument, the Consumer interface accepts an argument of any data type

b. The Supplier interface produces a return value of any data type, the Consumer interface does not return any value

c. The Supplier interface basically produces a value of a particular data type while the Consumer interface operates on an input value

201. What is the output of the following code snippet?.

```
Predicate<Integer> numberChecker = (num) -> num > 20;
int input = 10;
System.out.println(input+" greater than
20:"+numberChecker.test(input)); //Line 1
input = 40;
System.out.println(input+" greater than
20:"+numberChecker.test(input)); //Line 2
```

Answer:

The above code snippet uses the built–in functional interface called `Predicate`. This interface accepts an argument of any data type and returns a `boolean` value. So, it is basically used to test a condition. Here, the code creates a `Predicate` called `numberChecker` that accepts an integer value. It is implemented via a lambda expression that checks whether the input number is greater than 20. Line 1 applies the `Predicate` on the value 10 while Line 2 applies the `Predicate` on the value 40. So, the code prints the following output:

```
10 greater than 20:false
40 greater than 20:true
```

202. Which in–built functional interface would you use to convert a String to uppercase?

Answer:

There is a built–in functional interface called `UnaryOperator`. It accepts an argument of any data type and returns a result of the same data type. It has a method called `apply` that operates on the input value. So, you can use this to convert a String to uppercase. The following code demonstrates this:

```
UnaryOperator<String> converter = str -> str.
toUpperCase();
System.out.println(converter.apply("hello world"));
```

Here, the code creates a `UnaryOperator` implementation called `converter` that operates on a String value. A lambda expression is used that converts the String to uppercase. So, this code prints the following output:

```
HELLO WORLD
```

203. Is the code below valid? Explain.

```
@FunctionalInterface
public interface Interface1 {
    public void doSomething();
}
public interface Interface2 extends Interface1{
    public void doSomethingElse();
}
```

Answer:

The code above declares a functional interface called `Interface1` with an abstract method called `doSomething`. It then defines another functional interface called `Interface2` that extends `Interface1` and has and abstract method called `doSomethingElse`. This code is perfectly valid. `Interface2` now has two abstract methods, doSomething() and doSomethingElse(). Since it is not marked with the `@FunctionalInterface` annotation, it is okay to have multiple abstract methods. Had the `@FunctionalInterface` annotation been used on `Interface2`, the code would have caused a compilation error.

204. Name some pre–Java 8 interfaces that are made functional interfaces by Java 8

Answer:

Prior to Java 8, there are some interfaces that already had a single abstract method. Java 8 has designated these interfaces as functional interfaces by specifying the @ FunctionalInterface annotation on them. So, the abstract methods in these interfaces can be implemented via lambda expressions. These interfaces are as follows:

a. java.lang.Runnable – Used to create a Thread

b. java.util.cocurrent.Callable – Used to create a Thread that returns a value

c. java.util.Comparator – Used to compare values

d. java.io.FileFilter – Used to filter Files

205. Why are primitive specializations of the in–built functional interfaces like IntSupplier, BooleanSupplier, etc. added by Java 8?

Answer:

The primitive specializations of the in–built functional interfaces like IntSupplier, BooleanSupplier, etc. are added by Java to improve performance. The primitive specializations do away with the need for autoboxing and hence improve performance. The following code demonstrates this:

```
Supplier<Integer> integerSupplier = () -> new
Integer(new Random().nextInt());
```

This code creates a Supplier that returns a random integer less than 100. Since the primitive specialization is not used, the value returned by Random class needs to be wrapped as an Integer.

Now consider the following code:

```
IntSupplier integerSupplier2 = () -> new Random().
nextInt();
```

In this case an `IntSupplier` which is the primitive specialization of `Supplier` that returns an integer is used. So, there is no need to wrap the return value as an `Integer`. Since autoboxing is avoided, this code results in better performance.

206. Where are the built-in functional interfaces commonly used?

Answer:

lk operations on Collections. The built-in functional interfaces are commonly used as parameters to the methods in the stream API. The Stream methods apply the operation specified by the functional interface to each element in the Stream. For example, the Stream interface has a `filter` method that filters a Collection based on some condition. The condition is specified via the `Predicate` interface which is an in-built functional interface. It checks if each value in the input Stream matches the condition specified by the `Predicate`. Similarly, the Stream interface has a method called `map` that transforms the elements in a Stream. It accepts as parameter a `Function` instance which is an in-built functional interface. It applies the operation specified by the `Function` interface to each element in the Stream

Lambda Expressions

207. What is a lambda expression? What are the benefits of using lambda expressions?

Answer:

A lambda expression is used to specify a function without a name. It is used to implement the abstract method within a functional interface. Lambda expressions have several benefits as follows:

a. They make code concise. Prior to Java 8, developers had to write a lot of code to implement an interface which made the code lengthy and verbose. Lambda expressions get rid of most of the boilerplate code associated with implementing an interface

b. They allow passing around code as method arguments

c. They allow providing different implementation for the same method on the fly

d. Some of the other new features added by Java 8 like for–
each and Streams also use lambda expressions

208. How are lambda expressions and functional interfaces related to each other?

Answer:

A functional interface is an interface with a single abstract
method. A lambda expression is used to implement the abstract
method specified in the functional interface.

Functional interfaces were added by Java 8 to support lambda
expressions and add functional programming support to Java.
Since Java is an object–oriented language, lambda expressions
cannot be written on their own. They need to be associated
with an object. So, Java 8 introduced functional interfaces and
made it compulsory for lambda expressions to be used only
with functional interfaces. By making a lambda expression
implement a functional interface method, the lambda
expression becomes an implementation of the functional
interface. Functional interfaces and lambda expressions
together help to write clean and concise Java code.

209. Explain the syntax of a lambda expression

Answer:

The following is the syntax of a lambda expression:

```
(parameters) -> {lambda body}
```

So, a lambda expression consists of the **parameters** to the
expression, the **lambda operator (–>)** and the **expression body**.
A lambda expression can receive zero or more parameters. If it

does not accept any parameters, an empty parenthesis needs to be used. If it accepts a single parameter, the parameter need not be specified in parenthesis. If it accepts multiple parameters, they need to be specified in parenthesis and separated by commas. The lambda body is ordinary Java code and can contain any number of statements. If there is a single statement in the lambda body, the curly braces around the body may be skipped, otherwise they need to be specified.

210. Give some examples of lambda expressions

Answer:

The following are some examples of lambda expressions:

Example 1: Single Parameter, No Return Value

```
str -> System.out.println(str);
```

This lambda expression accepts one parameter and uses a `Sysout` statement to print it. It does not return any value.

Example 2: Multiple parameters and a return value

```
(num1,num2) -> num1+num2;
```

This lambda expression accepts two parameters and returns the result of adding them. The `return` keyword is not specified explicitly here.

Example 3: No parameter, lambda body and return value:

```
() ->{
   //doing something here
   return 0;
}
```

This lambda expression does not accept any parameters. It has a body that executes some code. It returns the value 0.

211. Write a code sample that creates a Functional interface and use a Lambda expression to implement it

Answer:

A functional interface is an interface with just one abstract method. Consider the following functional interface:

```
@FunctionalInterface
public interface StringConverter {
    public String convert(String s);
}
```

This code defines a functional interface called `StringConverter` with a method called `convert`. The `convert` method accepts a String value and returns a String. A lambda expression provides an implementation for the method in the functional interface.

So, you can then implement StringConverter interface using a lambda expression as follows:

```
StringConverter converter = (str) -> str.toUpperCase();
```

Here, the `StringConverter` is implemented via a lambda expression that converts the input String to uppercase and returns it.

212. Explain with a code sample how the same functional interface can be implemented differently using different lambda expressions

Answer:

Consider the following `StringConverter` functional interface:

```
@FunctionalInterface
public interface StringConverter {
   public String convert(String s);
}
```

Different implementations can now be provided for the `convert` methods via different lambda expressions as follows:

```
StringConverter upperCaseconverter = str -> str.
toUpperCase();
String result = upperCaseconverter.convert("Hello");
```

Here, the `StringConverter` interface is implemented via a lambda expression that converts the input String to uppercase and returns it.

Now consider the following code:

```
StringConverter lowerCaseconverter = str -> str.
toLowerCase();
String result = lowerCaseconverter.convert("Hello");
```

Here, the `StringConverter` interface is implemented via a lambda expression that converts the input String to lowercase and return it.

So different lambda expressions provide different implementations for the `StringConverter` interface.

213. Identify the error in the following lambda expression and how it can be fixed

```
(str) -> return str.toUpperCase();
```

Answer:

The above lambda expression uses the `return` keyword in the lambda body. If the `return` keyword is used, the lambda body needs to be included in curly brackets. Alternative, the `return` keyword can also be removed in order to get rid of the error. So, the above lambda expression can be fixed in either of the following ways:

```
(str) -> {return str.toUpperCase();};
```

or

```
(str) -> str.toUpperCase();
```

214. Is the following code valid? Explain

```java
public void generateSquareRoot(int num) {
    Function<Integer,Double> squareRoot = (num) ->
    Math.sqrt(num);
}
```

Answer:

The code above specifies a method called generateSquareRoot. It accepts as parameter an integer value. It then uses the in–built functional interface Function and implements it via a lambda expression. The code is not valid and causes a compilation error. This is because, you cannot declare a parameter or a local variable within a lambda expression that has the same name as a variable in the enclosing method. The generateSquareRoot method accepts a parameter called num and uses this same name in the lambda expression which causes the compilation error. It can be fixed by renaming either the method parameter or the lambda expression parameter to something else.

215. Write a functional interface for which the following lambda expression would work

```
(input) -> input.toUpperCase();
```

Answer:

The above code snippet specifies a lambda expression that accepts a String value, converts it to uppercase and returns it. So, it can be used to implement the following functional interface:

```
@FunctionalInterface
public interface Interface1 {
    public String doSomething(String input);
}
```

This code defines a functional interface called `Interface1`. It has a `doSomething` method that accepts as input a String and returns a String value.

216. Explain how you can create a new Thread using lambda expression.

Answer:

The `java.lang.Runnable` interface is used to create a new thread. Java 8 has designated this interface as a functional interface and so you can implement it using a lambda expression. The following code demonstrates this:

```
Runnable r = () -> {
    System.out.println("Starting Thread..");
    //some more code
};
Thread myThread = new Thread(r);
myThread.start();
```

Here, the `Runnable` interface is implemented via a lambda expression that has a simple `Sysout` statement. A new Thread object called `myThread` is created with this `Runnable` instance. The `myThread.start()` method is invoked which then spawns a new Thread.

Streams

217. Explain the different ways in which you can create a Stream.

Answer:

There are several ways in which you can create a Stream. These are as follows:

a. You can directly create a list from a List of values as follows:

```
Stream<String> values = String.of ("Red, "Blue");
```

b. You can create a Stream from a collection as follows:

```
List<Integer> numbers = Arrays.asList(1,2,3,4);
Stream<Integer> stream = numbers.stream();
```

c. You can create a Stream from an array as follows:

```
int[] numbers = new int[] {1,2,3,4};
IntStream arrayStream= Arrays.stream(numbers);
```

218. Explain the Stream filter operation with a code sample.

Answer:

The `Stream.filter()` operation can be used to filter a Stream based on some condition. So, it creates a new Stream that consists of only those elements that match the specified condition. It accepts as parameter a `Predicate` instance and filters the elements in the stream based on the specified predicate. The following code demonstrates this:

```
Stream<Integer> numbers = Stream.of(7,3,9,6,1);
Stream<Integer> output = numbers.filter(num -> num > 5);
```

This code creates a Stream of some Integer values. It then invokes the `filter()` method with a lambda expression that checks if the input number is greater than 5. So, the output Stream will only consist of those numbers that are greater than 5.

219. Explain the types of Stream operations.

Answer:

Stream operations can be categorized as follows:

a. **Intermediate** – Intermediate operations operate on Streams and produce a Stream output. Since intermediate operations produce a Stream, they can be chained to perform a series of operations. Some examples of intermediate operations are `filter`, `map`, `sorted`.

b. **Terminal** – Terminal operations operate on Streams but produce a non–stream result. So, they can produce a result of any data type. Terminal operations cannot be chained. When a number of Stream operations are chained, a terminal operation is typically the last operation. Some examples of terminal operations are count, `anyMatch`, `allMatch`, `collect`.

220. What is a parallel stream? Explain with a code sample how you can create a parallel stream.

Answer:

In addition to sequential streams, the Stream API also supports parallel streams. Parallel streams operate concurrently on the elements in a Stream and hence provide a performance improvement. A new method called `parallelStream()` has been added to the Collection interface. This can be used to obtain a parallel stream corresponding to the underlying collection. The following code demonstrates this:

```
List<String> colours = Arrays.
asList("Red","Green","Blue");
Stream<String> parallelStream = colours.
parallelStream();
```

This code first creates a List of String values called `colours`. It then invokes the `parallelStream()` method on the `colours` List. This returns a parallel stream corresponding to the List. Any further Stream operations performed on this stream will be executed concurrently on the elements in the Stream

221. How can you convert a Stream back to a Collection?

Answer:

The Stream interface has a method called `collect()`. This can be used to convert a Stream back to a Collection. The following code demonstrates this:

```
Stream<Integer> numbers = Stream.of(7,3,9,6,1);

List<Integer> filteredList = numbers.filter(num -> num >
5).collect(Collectors.toList());
```

This code first creates a List of Integers. It then invokes the filter() method to obtain the numbers that are greater than 5. After that, it invokes the collect() method. The collect() method accepts as parameter a Collector. The Collectors.toList() method is invoked which returns a Collector that converts the input Stream to a List. So, the filteredList is a List that has only the numbers that are greater than 5 from the input List. There are other methods in the Collectors class like Collectors.toSet, Collectors.toMap, Collectors.toCollection which can be used to convert the Stream to other types of Collections.

222. What is the output of the following code snippet?

```
Stream<Integer> numbers = Stream.of(10,15,20,25);
boolean anyMatch = numbers.anyMatch(num -> num%2==0);
System.out.println(anyMatch);
```

Answer:

The code snippet above uses the anyMatch() method on the Stream Interface. This method returns true if any of the elements in the input Stream match the specified condition. In this case, it checks if there is an even number in the input Stream. Since there are even numbers in the Stream, the anyMatch() method returns a true. So, this code prints the following output:

```
true
```

223. What is the difference between a Stream and a Collection?

Answer:

There are several differences between a Stream and a Collection. These are as follows:

a. Collections actually store the data. A stream on the other hand does not store any data, it just performs some operations on the underlying data

b. When you perform an operation on a Collection, the Collection gets modified. When you perform an operation on a Stream obtained on a Collection, the underlying Collection does not get modified

c. A Collection can be modified after it is created. A Stream on the other hand cannot be modified after it is constructed

d. You can traverse a Collection any number of times. However, you can traverse a Stream only once. If you wish to traverse over a Stream again it is not possible, you need to create a new Stream from the underlying source and traverse again

224. Suppose you have a List of String values. You want to create a new List that eliminates the duplicates from the original List and has the String values in uppercase. How will you achieve this via Stream operations?

Answer:

The following code snippet demonstrates the above requirement:

```
List<String> fruits = Arrays.
asList("Apple","Mango","Banana","Apple",
"Orange","Mango","Strawberry"); //Line 1
List<String> uniqueFruits = fruits.stream().distinct().
map(str -> str.toUpperCase()).collect(Collectors.
toList()); //Line 2
uniqueFruits.forEach(str -> System.out.println(str));//
Line 3
```

This code first creates a List of String values called `fruits` at Line 1. Line 2 first invokes the `fruits.stream()` which obtains a Stream on the `fruits` List. It then invokes the `distinct()` operation. The `distinct()` method returns a new Stream that consists of only the distinct elements in the input Stream. Next, it invokes the `map()` operation. The `map()` operation can be used to transform a Stream. It accepts as parameter a `Function` instance and applies the `Function` to each element in the Stream. Here, a lambda expression is used to convert each String in the Stream to uppercase. Finally, it invokes the `collect()` method, passing in a `Collector` that converts the Stream to a List. Line 3 then prints all the elements in the `uniqueFruits` List. So, this code prints the following output:

```
APPLE
MANGO
BANANA
ORANGE
STRAWBERRY
```

225. Is it possible to convert an array to a Stream? Explain

Answer:

Yes, it is possible to convert an Array to a Stream. Java 8 has added a `stream()` method to the `java.util.Arrays` class. This has many overloaded versions that accept arrays of different data types and convert the array to a Stream. The following code demonstrates converting an Integer array to a Stream:

```
int[] numbers = {10,20,30};
IntStream numberStream = Arrays.stream(numbers);
```

This code first creates an `int` array called `numbers`. It then uses the `Arrays.stream` method passing it the input array. The `Arrays.Stream` method returns an `IntStream` which is a primitive specialization of the Stream interface. Just like `IntStream`, Java 8 has also added `DoubleStream` and `LongStream` which are returned when the `Arrays.stream` method is invoked with a `double` or `long` array respectively.

226. Suppose you have an Employee class as follows:

```
public class Employee {
    private String name;
    private int salary;
}
```

And suppose you have a List of Employee objects as follows:

```
List<Employee> employees = new ArrayList<Employee>();
employees.add(new Employee("John",10000));
employees.add(new Employee("Ana",15000));
employees.add(new Employee("Tia",8000));
```

How can you create a new List is sorted based on the Employee salary using Streams?

Answer:

The following code can be used to create a new List sorted based on the Employee salary:

```
List<Employee> sortedList = employees.stream().
sorted((emp1,emp2) -> emp1.getSalary()-emp2.
getSalary()).collect(Collectors.toList());

sortedList.forEach(emp -> System.out.println(emp.
getSalary()));
```

This code first obtains a Stream on the `employees` List. It
then invokes the `sorted()` operation. The `sorted()` method
accepts as input a `Comparator`. Here, the `Comparator`
is implemented via a lambda expression that compares
the `salary` fields of the `Employee` objects. Finally, the
`collect()` method is invoked to convert the Stream back to a
List. So, this code prints the following output:

```
8000
10000
15000
20000
```

Method References

227. What is a method reference? What are the benefits of method references?

Answer:

A method reference is a new operator introduced by Java 8. It is a shortcut operator for a lambda expression. It is represented by the :: symbol.

Method references have several benefits as follows:

a. **They avoid code duplication** – Sometimes, your code may already have a method that has the same code that you would like to specify in a lambda expression. In such a scenario method references are useful. So instead of re-writing the code again in the lambda expression, you can refer to the existing method via a method reference.

b. **They make code concise** – Method references are a step further from lambda expression. They help to make the code even more concise by moving the code from the lambda expression into a separate method.

228. What are the different types of method references?

Answer:

There are 4 types of method references. These are as follows:

a. **Static method reference** – This occurs when a static method of a class is referenced via the method reference operator. Its syntax is as follows:

```
class::staticmethod
```

b. **Instance method reference** – This occurs when an instance method of a class is referenced via the method reference operator. Its syntax is as follows:

```
object::instancemethod
```

c. **Constructor reference** – This occurs when a constructor of a class is referenced via the method reference operator. Its syntax is as follows:

```
class::new
```

d. **Arbitrary method reference** – This occurs when an instance method of a class is accessed but not on any specific object. Its syntax is as follows:

```
class::instancemethod
```

229. Give an example of static method reference.

Answer:

Static method reference occurs when a static method of a class is accessed via the method reference operator. The following code demonstrates this:

```
public class MethodReferenceDemo {
    public static boolean checkIfNumberGreaterThan8(int
    num) {
        return num > 8;
    }
public static void main(String[] args) {
        Predicate<Integer> numberChecker =
        MethodReferenceDemo::checkIfNumberGreaterThan8;
        boolean flag = numberChecker.test(10);
    }
}
```

Here, the `MethodReferenceDemo` class has a static method called `checkIfNumberGreaterThan8()`. This checks if the input number is greater than 8 and returns a boolean value accordingly. In the main method, a `Predicate` is defined. However, instead of using a lambda expression to implement the `Predicate`, the existing `checkIfNumberGreaterThan8()` is referenced via the method reference operator. Since `checkIfNumberGreaterThan8()` is a static method, the class name followed by method name is used.

230. Consider the following Shape class:

```
public class Shape {
    private String name;
}
```

What changes are required in this class in order to make the code below valid?

```
List<String> shapeNames = Arrays.
asList("Circle","Triangle");

List<Shape> shapes = shapeNames.stream().
map(Shape::new).collect(Collectors.toList());
```

Answer:

The code above creates a List of String values called shapeNames. It then uses the Stream map() operation to create a List of Shape objects called shapes. The code uses a constructor reference to create a new Shape object using the String shape name. So, the Shape class requires a constructor that accepts a String value as input as follows:

```
public Shape(String name) {
    this.name = name;
}
```

231. Explain what type of method reference is String::toUpperCase

Answer:

String::toUpperCase is an example of arbitrary method reference. It refers to the toUpperCase method of the String class but not on any specific object. This is generally used while iterating through a Collection or a Stream. For example, suppose you want to convert all the elements of a List to uppercase. You can use this String::toUppercase as follows:

```
List<String> colours = Arrays.
asList("Red","Blue","Green");

    List<String> upperCaseColours =
colours.stream().map(String::toUpperCase).
collect(Collectors.toList());
```

DateTime API

232. Explain what is wrong in the following code snippet and how you can fix it

```
LocalDate date1 = LocalDate.of(2018, 7, 24);
LocalTime time1 = date1.atTime(5, 30);
```

Answer:

The code snippet above first creates a LocalDate called date1. It then uses the atTime() method on date1 and assigns the result to a LocalTime object called time1. This causes a compilation error. The atTime() method combines the date in the current time object with the specified time and returns a LocalDateTime object. So, you can fix the code above by making the following change:

```
LocalDateTime time1 = date1.atTime(5, 30);
```

This combines the date specified in date1 with the time **5:30** and returns a `LocalDateTime` object.

233. Explain with appropriate code samples the different ways in which you can create a LocalDate

Answer:

The LocalDate class has some static methods using for LocalDate creation. These are as follows:

a. Creating a LocalDate corresponding to the current Date – The `LocalDate.now()` method can be used for this as shown below:

```
LocalDate date1 = LocalDate.now();
```

b. Creating a LocalDate corresponding to the specified year, month and day – The `LocalDate.of` method can be used for this as shown below:

```
LocalDate date2 = LocalDate.of(2018, 7, 24);
```

c. Creating a LocalDate corresponding to a String Date – The `LocalDate.parse` can be used for this as shown below:

```
LocalDate date3 = LocalDate.parse("2014-08-11");
```

234. Explain with a code sample how you can check if a date is before another date

Answer:

The `LocalDate` class has a method called `isBefore()`. You can use this to check if a date is before another date as shown below:

```
LocalDate date1 = LocalDate.of(2018, 7, 24);
LocalDate date2 = LocalDate.parse("2014-08-11");
boolean isBefore = date1.isBefore(date2);
System.out.println("isBefore:"+isBefore);
```

This code creates two date objects, date1 and date2. It invokes isBefore() on date1, passing date2 as an argument. Since date1 is after date2, the isBefore() method returns false. So, this code prints the output shown below:

```
isBefore:false
```

235. Explain the ZonedDateTime class

Answer:

The ZonedDateTime class represents a date and time that also has a time–zone information. So, in addition to the year, month, day, hour, minutes, seconds and nano seconds components, it also has a ZoneId component. The ZoneId is an instance of the java.time.ZoneId and represents the time–zone. There are about 40 time zones that can be represented via a Zone Id. The code below shows how you can create a ZonedDateTime:

```
ZoneId zoneId = ZoneId.of("Asia/Kolkata");
ZonedDateTime zonedDateTime = ZonedDateTime.now(zoneId);
```

So, the above code snippet first creates a ZoneId corresponding to **Asia/Calcutta** which is the IST time–zone. It then creates a ZonedDateTime that corresponding to the current time as per the system clock but with this zone id.

236. What will be the output of the following code snippet?

```
LocalTime localTime = LocalTime.of(7, 15);
System.out.println(localTime.minusMinutes(30));
```

Answer:

The above code creates a `LocalTime` instance. A `LocalTime` represents time that has the hours, minutes, seconds and nanoseconds component. Here a `LocalTime` object is created corresponding to **7:15**. The code then invokes the `minusMinutes()` method with the value **30** and prints the output. The `minusMinutes()` method subtracts the specified number of minutes from the LocalTime on which it is invoked. After subtracting **30** minutes from **7:15**, the time would be **6:45**. So this code prints the output shown below:

```
06:45
```

237. How can you obtain the day of the week corresponding to a date using the Java 8 DateTime API?

Answer:

The `LocalDate` class has a method called `getDayOfWeek()`. You can use this to get the day of the week corresponding to a Date as shown by the code below:

```
LocalDate date = LocalDate.parse("2017-04-25");
System.out.println(date.getDayOfWeek());
```

The above code creates a `LocalDate` corresponding to **25th April 2017**. It then invokes the `getDayOfWeek()` method on this date object. This method returns an `enum` called `DayOfWeek`. The `DayOfWeek` enum has values corresponding to each day of the week. Since the date **25th April 2017** corresponds to a **Tuesday**, the `getDayOfWeek` method returns an enum value corresponding to **Tuesday**. So, this code prints the output shown below:

```
TUESDAY
```

238. Explain the differences between the Period and Duration class

Answer:

The Period and Duration are both classes introduced by the DateTime API and represent a time duration. However, there are some differences between the two. These are as follows:

a. A Period represents a time interval in years, months and days. A Duration on the other hand represents a time interval in seconds and nanoseconds

b. A Period is used to measure the time interval between two LocalDate objects. A Duration on the other hand is used to measure the time interval between two LocalTime objects

c. A Period is typically used to measure longer time intervals whereas a Duration is used to measure shorter time intervals

239. Suppose you have a String date in the yyyy/mm/dd format. How can you obtain a LocalDate object corresponding to such a date?

Answer:

The code below demonstrates converting a String date in yyyy/mm/dd format to a `LocalDate`:

```
String strDate = "2012/10/11";
LocalDate date = LocalDate.
parse(strDate,DateTimeFormatter. ofPattern("yyyy/MM/
dd"));
System.out.println(date);
```

The `LocalDate` has a `parse()` method which can be used
to convert a String Date to a `LocalDate` object. The `parse()`
method accepts a `LocalDate` in the **yyyy–MM–dd** format.
In the scenario above, the date is in the `yyyy/MM/dd` format,
so parse() method will not work as it is. However, there is
an overloaded version of the parse() method which accepts
a `DateTimeFormatter` instance in addition to the String
date. A `DateTimeFormatter` can be created via the static
`DateTimeFormatter.ofPattern()` method. This method
accepts as parameter a String corresponding to the desired data
format. Here, the code creates a `DateTimeFormatter` that
can parse a date in the **yyyy/mm/dd** format. So, this code prints
the output shown below:

```
2012-10-11
```

240. What is the output of the following code snippet?

```
LocalDateTime dateTime = LocalDateTime.parse("2014-12-
28T08:45:00");
dateTime = dateTime.withYear(1998);
System.out.println(dateTime);
```

Answer:

The code above first creates a `LocalDateTime` instance.
It then invokes the `dateTime.withYear()` method. This
method updates the year component on the `LocalDateTime`
on which it is invoked to the specified year. So, in this case, it
updates the year in `dateTime` to **1998** and assigns the result

to the dateTime object. So, this code prints the output shown below:

```
1998-12-28T08:45
```

241. Explain how you can find out if a year is a leap year using the new DateTime API

Answer:

There is a method called isLeapYear() on the LocalDate class. This can be used to check if a year is a leap year as demonstrated by the code below:

```
LocalDate date1 = LocalDate.of(2020, 7, 24);
boolean isLeapYear = date1.isLeapYear();
```

This code creates a LocalDate called date1 and then invokes the isLeapYear() method on date1. The isLeapYear() method returns a **boolean** value. In this case, since date1 corresponds to the year **2020** which is a leap year, the isLeapYear() method will return true.

Static and Default Interface Methods

242. What are static and default methods? Why were they introduced by Java 8?

Answer:

Before Java 8, interfaces could only have abstract methods. So, they could not have methods with method bodies. Java 8 allows interfaces to have methods with method bodies as static and default methods. These were added for the following reasons:

a. Default interface methods help to keep code backward compatible. Prior to Java 8, if a new method was added to an interface, all the classes that implement the interface needed to be modified. Default methods overcome this restriction. So, they allow you to add a method with a method body in the interface. So, all implementing classes do not need to be modified

b. Static interface methods help to group together utility methods. Static interface methods cannot be overridden in the classes that implement the method. So, this avoids unwanted results due of incorrect implementation and provides an additional level of security.

243. What is the difference between an abstract class and an interface after Java 8?

Answer:

The addition of Java 8 default interface methods has reduced the distinction between abstract classes and interfaces. Prior to Java 8, interfaces could not have concrete methods. However, Java 8 has added default and static methods in interfaces. These are methods that have a method body. This has further reduced the distinction between abstract classes and interfaces. However, there are there some differences between the two. These are as follows:

a. Abstract classes can have instance fields. Interfaces on the other hand cannot have instance fields. So basically, an abstract class can have a state via an instance field, whereas an interface cannot have state

b. Abstract class can have a constructor and can be instantiated. Interface on the other hand cannot have a constructor

244. Write a code sample that demonstrates a default method

Answer:

A default method is simply a method with a method body within an interface. It has the `default` keyword. The following code demonstrates this:

```
public interface MyInterface {
   public void doSomething();
   public default void doSomethingElse() {
      System.out.println("Doing something else....");
   }
}
```

This code has declared an interface called `MyInterface`. It has an abstract method called `doSomething()` and a default method called `doSomethingElse()`. The default method has the **default** keyword specified. It has a method body.

245. What is the difference between a static and a default interface method?

Answer:

Both static and default interface methods have a method body. However, there are some differences between the two:

a. A static method has the static keyword specified, while the default method has the default keyword specified

b. Default interface methods can be overridden. Static methods on the other hand cannot be overridden

c. Default methods can be invoked via an object of the class that implements the interface. Static interface methods on the other hand cannot be invoked via the class or object of the class that implements the interface. They need to be invoked via the interface name

246. Identify the error in the following code snippet and explain how it can be fixed

```
public interface MyInterface {
    public static void doSomething() {
        System.out.println("Doing something....");
    }
}
public class MyClass implements MyInterface{
    public static void main(String args[]) {
        MyClass obj = new MyClass();
        obj.doSomething();  //Line 1
    }
}
```

Answer:

The code above defines an interface called `MyInterface` with a `static` method called `doSomething()`. It then creates a class called `MyClass` which implements `MyInterface`. The `main` method of `MyClass` creates an object of `MyClass` called `obj` and invokes the `doSomething()` method at Line 1. This causes a compilation error at Line 1. This is because the code tries to access a static interface method via an object of the class. Static interface methods can only be accessed via the interface name. In order to fix the error, Line 1 needs to be replaced as follows:

```
MyInterface.doSomething();
```

Optionals

247. What is an Optional and why was it added by Java 8?

Answer:

An Optional is used to represent a value that can either be present or absent. It has methods that can be used to retrieve the underlying value if present. The following code demonstrates an Optional:

```
Optional<Integer> number;
```

So here, `number` is an optional of type `Integer`. It may or may not contain a value.

Optionals were added by Java 8 to avoid the boilerplate code associated with null checks. Sometimes, a method may return a null. This can result in a `NullPointerException`. In order to avoid the exception, the code that invokes the method needs to have explicit null checks. This can make the code difficult to read. Java 8 Optionals help to avoid this boilerplate code. So instead of having an explicit null check, an optional can be used. If the value is present it can be retrieved.

248. How can an Optional be created?

Answer:

There are some static methods on the Optional class which can be used to create an Optional. These are as follows:

a. `Optional.isEmpty` – This creates an empty Optional, that is an Optional without a value as shown below:

```
Optional<Integer> number = Optional.empty();
```

b. `Optional.of` – This creates an Optional with a particular value as shown below:

```
Optional<Integer> number = Optional.of(10); //creates
Optional with the value 10
```

c. `Optional.ofNullable` – This creates an Optional with either a null or a non–null value as shown below:

```
Optional<Integer> number = Optional.ofNullable(10); //
creates Optional with the value 10
```

It can also be used to create an Optional with a null value as follows:

```
Optional<Integer> number = Optional.ofNullable(null);
```

249. Explain the Optional.ifPresent method with a code sample

Answer:

The `Optional.ifPresent` method performs an operation on the value in the Optional if it is present. The operation to be performed is specified as a `Consumer` instance. If the Optional is empty, it does not do anything. The following code demonstrates this:

```
Optional<String> strOptional = Optional.of("Test");
strOptional.ifPresent(str -> System.out.println(str.
toUpperCase()));
```

This code creates an Optional `strOptional` corresponding to the value **Test**. The `ifPresent` method is then invoked with a lambda expression that converts the value in the Optional to uppercase and prints it. So, this code prints the following output:

```
TEST
```

In case, the input Optional is empty, the `ifPresent()` method does not do anything.

250. What is the difference between the orElse and orElseThrow method?

Answer:

Both the `orElse()` and `orElseThrow()` are methods on the Optional class. If a value is present in the Optional, they return the value. They differ in what happens when a value is not present in the Optional.

The `orElse()` method accepts as parameter a value and returns this value if invoked on an empty Optional. The following code demonstrates this:

```
Optional<String> strOptional1 = Optional.empty();
String strValue1 = strOptional1.
orElse("Default");
```

Here, since `strOptional1` is an empty Optional, the

`orElse()` method returns the value **Default**.

The `orElseThrow()` method throws an Exception if invoked on an empty Optional. It accepts as parameter a `Supplier` instance that returns an Exception. The following code demonstrates this:

```
Optional<String> strOptional2 = Optional.empty();
String strValue2 = strOptional1.orElseThrow(() -> new
IllegalArgumentException());
```

Here, since `strOptional2` is an empty Optional, the `orElseThrow()` method throws an `IllegalArgumentException`

251. What will be the output of the following code snippet?

```
Optional<Integer> opInt1 = Optional.of(200); //Line 1
Optional<Integer> opInt2 = opInt.filter(num -> num >
100); //Line 2
System.out.println(opInt2.get()); //Line 3
```

Answer:

The Optional class has a method called `filter()` which is used in the code snippet above. The `filter()` method accepts as `Predicate` and applies the `Predicate` to the value in the Optional if present. If the condition in the `Predicate` is satisfied, it returns the value in the Optional, otherwise it returns an empty Optional. In this case, Line 1 creates an Integer Optional with the value **200**. Line 2 invokes the `filter()` method with a `Predicate` that checks if the value in the Optional is greater than **100**. Since this is true, the `filter()` method returns an Optional with the value **100** which is assigned to `opInt2`. So, the `get()` method returns this value. So, this code prints the following output:

```
100
```

Collection
Improvements

08

252. Explain with a code sample how the forEach method works

Answer:

Java 8 has added a new default method called forEach to the Iterable interface. The java.util.Collection interface extends the Iterable interface and so the forEach method is available to all the Collection classes. The forEach method helps to internally iterate through a Collection without an explicit for loop. The following code demonstrates this:

```
List<String> colours = Arrays.asList("Red","Blue","Black
","White");
colours.forEach(str -> System.out.println(str));
```

This code declares a List of String values called colours. The forEach() method is then invoked on this List. The forEach() method accepts as parameter a Consumer instance and operates on it. In this case, the `Consumer` is implemented via a lambda expression that simply prints the value passed to it. So, this code prints the following output:

```
Red
Blue
Black
White
```

253. What are some of the improvements made by Java 8 on the List interface?

Answer:

Java 8 has added some methods to the List interface as follows:

a. `List.sort` – Java 8 has added the `List.sort` method. This can be used to sort a List. It accepts as parameter a `Comparator` and sorts the input List as per the specified `Comparator`.

b. `List.replaceAll` – Java 8 has added the `List.replaceAll` method. This can be used to replace all the values in a List. It accepts as parameter a `UnaryOperator` interface. `UnaryOperator` is a specialization of the `Function` interface that accepts an input of a particular data type and returns a result of the same data type. The `replaceAll()` method applies the `UnaryOperator` to each element in the List.

254. How does the Map.getOrDefault method work?

Answer:

Java 8 has added the `getOrDefault` method to the Map interface. It accepts as parameter the key whose value needs to be retrieved as well as a default value. So, it returns a value corresponding to the specified key if present, otherwise, it returns the default value passed in. The following code snippet demonstrates this:

```
Map<Integer,String> fruits = new
HashMap<Integer,String>();

fruits.put(1,"Apple");

fruits.put(2,"Orange");

String fruit1 = fruits.getOrDefault(1,"Mango"); //
returns apple

String fruit2 = fruits.getOrDefault(3,"Mango"); //
returns mango
```

This code creates a map called fruits with an Integer key and a String value. It adds some values to the map. It first uses the getOrDefault method to retrieve the value corresponding to the key **1** passing the default value as **Mango**. Since there is a value in the Map with key **1**, fruit1 is assigned the value corresponding to the key which is **Apple**. It first uses the getOrDefault method to retrieve the value corresponding to the key **3** passing the default value as **Mango**. Since there is no value in the map with key **3**, fruit2 is assigned the default value **Mango**

255. What is the output of the following code snippet?

```
Map<Integer,String> fruits = new
HashMap<Integer,String>();
fruits.put(1,"Apple");
fruits.put(2,"Orange");
fruits.put(3,"Strawberry");
fruits.replace(1, "Mango"); //Line 1
fruits.replace(2, "Orange","Banana"); //Line 2
fruits.replace(3, "Blackberry","Pineapple"); //Line 3
System.out.println(fruits.get(1));
System.out.println(fruits.get(2));
System.out.println(fruits.get(3));
```

Answer:

This code prints the following output:

```
Mango
Banana
Strawberry
```

The `Map.replace(key,value)` method replaces a value only if it is mapped to a value. In the above example, the key **1** is mapped to the value **Apple**, so the `replace()` method replaces the value **Apple** with the value **Mango**. The `Map.replace(key, oldValue,newValue)` replaces a value only if it is mapped to the specified value. In the above example, the key **2** is mapped to the value **Orange**. So, the `replace` method at Line 2 replaces the value **Orange** with the value **Banana**. Also, the key **3** is mapped to the value **Strawberry**. So, the replace method at Line 3 does not replace the value since the key **3** is not mapped to **Blackberry**.

256. Explain the differences between an Iterator and SplitIterator

Answer:

Both the Iterator and SplitIterator can be used for iterating through the elements in a Collection. However, there are some differences between these interfaces. These are as follows:

a. The Iterator interface is present right from the earlier versions of Java. The SplitIterator is a new interface added by Java 8

b. The Iterator interface only supports sequential processing. The SplitIterator supports both sequential as well as parallel processing

c. The Iterator can be used for iterating over a Collection. The SplitIterator can be used for iterating over a Collection as well as a Stream.

d. The Iterator only allows traversing over the elements of a Collection individually. The SplitIterator on the other hand allows traversing over the elements of a Collection individually as well as in bulk

Miscellaneous

257. What are the advantages of CompletableFuture class over the Future Interface?

Answer:

Prior to Java 8, Java had the `Callable` class and the `Future` interface. These could be used to return the result of an asynchronous computation. However, the `Future` interface had several issues. The `CompletableFuture` overcomes all these issues as follows:

a. A `Future` cannot be completed manually. So, if a task is hung, there is no way of completing the task manually. `CompletableFuture` on the other hand has a method called `complete()` that allows completing a task manually

b. `Future` has a method called `get()` that returns the result of computation. However, this method blocks until the result becomes available. So, if you want to perform any computation on the result of the Future, you need to wait for the result to be available. A CompletableFuture on the other hand allows attaching callbacks to the result of a computation. These callbacks execute once the result is available, so there is no need to wait

c. The Future interface does not have any exception handling mechanism. The CompletableFuture on the other hand has a method called exceptionally() that allows running alternate code in case an exception occurs.

258. What is StringJoiner? Explain with a code sample

Answer:

StringJoiner is a new class added by Java 8. It helps to concatenate Strings separated by a delimiter and having a prefix and suffix. The following code demonstrates this:

```
StringJoiner strJoiner = new StringJoiner(":","[","]");
//Line 1
strJoiner.add("cat"); //Line 2
strJoiner.add("dog"); //Line 3
strJoiner.add("mouse"); //Line 4
System.out.println(strJoiner); //Line 5
```

This code creates a StringJoiner. It uses the colon symbol(:) as the delimiter and square brackets ([]) as the prefix and suffix. It then invokes the add() method with some String values. So this code prints the following output:

```
[cat:dog:mouse]
```

259. Explain the differences between the Comparator.reverse and Comparator.reverseOrder methods

Answer:

Both the `Comparator.reversed` and `Comparator.reverseOrder` are methods added by Java 8 to the `Comparator` interface. Both help in sorting a Collection in reverse order. However, there are some differences between the two as follows:

a. `Comparator.reversed` is a default method while `Comparator.reverseOrder` is a static method

b. The `Comparator.reversed` requires a comparator to be present. It simply reverses that comparator. The `Comparator.reverseOrder` does not require a Comparator to be present. It directly returns a comparator that sorts in reverse order

c. The `Comparator.reversed` returns a Comparator that imposes the reverse ordering of the Comparator on which it is invoked. The `Comparator.reverseOrder` on the other hand returns a Comparator that imposes the reverse of the natural ordering of the elements in the Collection

260. **Identify the error in the code below and explain what needs to be done to fix it**

```
public class Employee {
    private String name;
    private double salary;
    //constructor, getters and setters
}
List<Employee> employees = new ArrayList<Employee>();
    employees.add(new Employee("A",10000));
    employees.add(new Employee("B",5000.50));
    employees.add(new Employee("C",15000));
    employees.sort(Comparator.comparingInt(employee ->
    employee.getSalary())); //Line 1
```

Answer:

The above code has a compilation error at Line 1. The employees.sort() method is used with the Comparator.comparingInt. This method accepts as parameter a ToIntFunction functional interface and sorts based on an int field. However, here a lambda expression that returns the salary value which is a double is used. So, this causes a compilation error. In order to fix this error, Line 1 needs to be modified as follows:

```
employees.sort(Comparator.comparingDouble(employee ->
employee.getSalary()));
```

Now, the Comparator.comparingDouble() method is used. This method accepts as parameter a ToDoubleFunction interface that compares based on a Double field.

261. Explain the differences between the CompletableFuture.runAsync and the CompletableFuture.supplyAsync methods

Answer:

Both the runAsync and the supplyAsync methods can be used to run code asynchronously. However, there are some differences between the two as follows:

a. The runAsync method does not return a result, so it returns a CompletableFuture<Void>. The supplyAsync method on the other hand returns a value from the thread. So, it returns a CompletableFuture<T>

b. The runAsync method accepts as parameter a Runnable instance. The supplyAsync method on the other hand accepts as parameter a Supplier instance.

c. The `runAsync` method executes the code in the `Runnable` implementation in a separate thread. The `supplyAsync` method on the other hand executes the code in the `Supplier` in a separate Thread and returns the value produced by the `Supplier`

Modules

262. What is a module? What benefits do they offer?

Answer:

A module consists of a group of related packages. Just like you put a set of related classes into a package, you can put a set of related packages into a module. Modules offer several benefits as follows:

a. If an application has a large number of packages, it becomes difficult to keep track. Modules come to the rescue, they help to organize packages, that is related packages can be grouped into a module

b. Modules can be deployed by themselves. So, this helps to reduce the size of an application

c. Modules offer better security. Before modules, the only way to make a class reusable in other packages was to make it public. However, this poses a security issue since public classes are accessible to everyone. Grouping packages into modules ensures that the class is not accessible outside the module.

d. Since there were no modules before Java 9, the Java API jar files like rt.jar were very big in size. Instead Java 9 has split this into smaller modules which are easier to test and maintain

e. Prior to Java 9, security was an issue as developers were able to access internal JDK files. Modules help to overcome this issue too. So with modules you can control which packages within the module are visible and accessible outside the module.

263. What is the module descriptor?

Answer:

A module descriptor is a Java file named module–info.java. It contains information about the module. It needs to be present at the root of the module. The following lines demonstrate the structure of the module descriptor:

```
module demomodule {
//optional directives
}
```

The module descriptor can contain some optional directives. Some of the directives that can be specified within the module descriptor are as follows:

a. **Name** – This specified the name of the module

b. **exports** – This specifies the names of the packages within this module that will be available to other modules.

c. **requires** – This specifies the names of the modules that the current module depends on. So if these modules are not specified, the current module may not work.

d. **provides** – This specifies the services that the current module provides. This directive should be used when a module acts as a service provider

e. **uses** –This specifies the services that the current module consumes. This directive should be used when the module is a service consumer

f. **open** – This specifies that the classes in the currently module can be accessed via Java reflection

264. What is the difference between a package and a module?

Answer:

Both packages and modules are a logical unit and encapsulate some Java files. However, there are several differences between the two as follows:

a. Packages are present right from the early versions of Java. Modules on the other had are added by Java 9

b. Packages were added by Java to avoid name clashes that it they allow having a class with the same name in different packages. Modules were added by Java to modularize the JDK and to improve security

c. A package contains a group of related files. A module on the other hand contains a group of related packages

d. A package does not require a package descriptor, a module requires a module descriptor called module–info.java

e. Packages cannot be deployed by themselves; modules can be deployed by themselves

f. The classes within a package are visible via reflection. The classes within a module are not visible via reflection unless the open directive is specified in the module descriptor

265. Explain the changes made to JDK for Java 9

Answer:

Java 9 has made some fundamental changes which takes advantage of modules. Prior to Java 9, after installing the JDK a folder called **jre\lib** was created. This had all the core jar files. When you install Java 9, the jre\lib folder is no longer created. Instead a folder called **jmods** is created in the root of the JDK installation. The **jmods** folder has modules corresponding to all the core Java files. So instead of having a big far rt.jar, JDK 9 has separate modules.

266. Consider the following code snippet:

```
package mypackage;
public class MyClass {
    public void doSomething() {
    }
}
```

In order for this code to be deployed as part of a module, what needs to be done?

Answer:

The code above specifies a class called MyClass as part of a package called mypackage. In order for this code above to be deployed as part of a module, a module descriptor needs to be created as follows:

```
module mymodule {
exports mypackage;
}
```

So, this specifies a module called `mymodule`. It uses the exports directive with the package `mypackage` indicating that `mypackage` will be available to other modules.

267. Explain the requires static module directive. When should it be used?

Answer:

The **requires static** directive is used to specify optional dependencies, that is dependencies that are required at compile time but not required at runtime. Suppose you have developed a module and require some third–party library which the end users of your module will never require. In such a case, you can specify the third–party library via the requires static directive while defining your module. So, the users of your module will need to have the third–party library at compile time, but they do not need it at runtime.

Stream/ Collection Improvements

268. What are some of the improvements made by Java 9 on the Stream Interface?

Answer:

The following are some of the improvements made by Java 9 on the Stream interface:

a. `Stream.ofNullable` – Java 9 has added a `Stream. ofNullable()` method on the Stream interface. This helps to create a Stream with a value that may be null. So, if a non–null value is passes to this method, it creates a Stream with that method, otherwise it creates an empty stream

b. `takeWhile, dropWhile` – Both the `takeWhile()` and `dropWhile()` methods operate on a Stream. They can be used to obtain a subset of the input Stream.

c. `Stream.iterate` – Java 9 has added an overloaded

version of the `Stream.iterate()` method that accepts a `Predicate` and terminates the Stream when the condition specified by the `Predicate` is true.

269. Is the code below valid? If not, what can be done to fix it?

```
Stream<String> strStream = Stream.of(null);
strStream.forEach(str -> System.out.println(str));
```

Answer:

The code above is valid and does not cause any compilation error. However, when it is executed, it will cause a `NullPointerException`. This is because you cannot create a Stream with a null value using the `Stream.of()` method. In order to fix the code above, you need to make the following change:

```
Stream<String> strStream = Stream.ofNullable(null);
strStream.forEach(str -> System.out.println(str));
```

Java 9 had added the `ofNullable()` method to the Stream interface that helps you create a Stream with a **null** value. So, the code above does not cause a NullPointerException.

270. Identify the issue in the code snippet below and explain how it can be fixed

```
List<Integer> numbers = List.of(5,10,15); //Line 1
numbers.add(20); //Line 2
System.out.println(numbers); //Line 3
```

Answer:

Java 9 has added a static method `of()` to all the Collection interfaces. The code above uses this method to create an Integer List at Line 1. The of method creates an immutable List which cannot be modified. However, Line 2 tries to add a value to the List which will cause an Exception when the code is executed. So, in order to fix the code above, you need remove Line 2. So, you need to re–write the code as follows:

```
List<Integer> numbers = List.of(5,10,15,20); //Line 1
System.out.println(numbers); //Line 3
```

271. Which Java 9 method can you use to create a Set of String values?

Answer:

Java 9 has added a static factory method to the Set interface. You can use this to create a Set with String values. The following code demonstrates this:

```
Set<String> months = Set.
of("January","February","March");
```

This code creates a Set of String values called `months`. It uses the `String.of()` method with the values specified. The `String.of()` has several overloaded versions that accept from 0 to 10 arguments as well as a version that accepts varargs.

272. What will be the output of the following code snippet?

```
Stream<Integer> oddNumbers = Stream.iterate(1,num ->
num <= 20, num -> num+2);
oddNumbers.forEach(num -> System.out.print(num+" "));
```

Answer:

Prior to Java 9, there was a `Stream.iterate()` method that created an infinite Stream of values. Java 9 has added an overloaded version of the `Stream.iterate()` method that creates a finite Stream. So, this method accepts an additional parameter which is a Predicate and stops the stream as soon as the Predicate is true. So, this code prints the following output:

```
1 3 5 7 9 11 13 15 17 19
```

Miscellaneous

273. What changes are made by Java 9 to interfaces and why?

Answer:

Java 9 allows private methods in interfaces. Before Java 8, interfaces could only have abstract methods. Java 8 added support for static and default interface methods. Default and static methods are nothing but interfaces with method bodies. Java 9 goes a step further and allows private methods in interfaces. Private interface methods allow reusing code. So, if an interface has several default and static methods and there is some common code across these methods, this code can be moved to a private method.

The following code demonstrates this:

```java
public interface Sample {
default method1(){
   //some code
   doSomething();
}
default method2(){
   //some code
   doSomething();
}
private void doSomething(){
     System.out.println("Doing something..");
  }
}
```

Here, the doSomething() is a private interface method that is used within the default methods method1() and method2().

274. What is JShell?

Answer:

Jshell is basically a command line tool. It allows you to write and run Java code without creating a class file. It can be launched by typing jshell on the command prompt. Once Jshell opens up, you can type in any Java code and JShell will display the output of the code. So, for example if you type the following:

```java
System.out.println("Hello World");
```

JShell will print the text **"Hello World"**.

JShell adds REPL support to Java. REPL stands for Read Evaluate Print Loop Many languages like Python also provide REPL capabilities.

275. What is the output of the following code snippet?

```
Optional<Double> myDoubleOptional = Optional.of(10.0);
Optional<Double> defaultOptional = Optional.of(50.0);
double value = myDoubleOptional.or(() ->
defaultOptional).get();
System.out.println(value);
```

Answer:

Java 9 has added a new method on the Optional class called
or(). This accepts as parameter a `Supplier` instance that
produces an Optional. It returns an Optional. So, if the
Optional on which it is invoked is a non–empty Optional,
it returns that Optional, otherwise it returns the Optional
generated by the passed Supplier. In the code snippet above,
the or method is invoked on `myDoubleOptional` which
is an Optional with the value **10**. Since this is a non–empty
Optional, the or method returns this value and not the
`defaultOptional`. So, this code prints the following output:

```
10.0
```

276. What changes has Java 9 made to the try–with statement?

Answer:

The try–with statement was added by Java 7. It allows
automatically closing resources without an explicit close
statement. So, for example if you are writing a file writing code,
if you use a try–with statement, the `FileWriter` gets closed
automatically once the try statement completes. The downside
of this was that the resource that needs to be automatically
closed needs to be part of the try statement. So, if a resource
is declared outside the try–with statement, it needs to be
declared again as part of the try–with. Java 9 does away with
this restriction. So, with Java 9, you can use a resource that is
declared outside the try–with statement within the try–with.

277. What is the use of the stream method added by Java 9 on the Optional class?

Answer:

The `stream()` method added by Java 9 on the Optional class can be used to convert an Optional into a Stream. This allows applying all the Stream operations on an Optional. The following code demonstrates this:

```
Optional<String> str = Optional.of("Hello");
Stream<String> strStream = str.stream();
```

This code defines an Optional called str which has a String value **Hello**. It then uses the `stream()` method. This converts the Optional to a Stream with one value. So now all Stream operations like `map`, `filter`, etc. can be applied on this stream.

278. Explain the ProcessHandle class and some of its important methods

Answer:

Java 9 has added a new class called `java.lang.ProcessHandle`. This helps to manage processes related to the operating system and helps to interact with the operating system. Some of the methods on this class are as follows:

a. `current()` – This is a static method that returns a `ProcessHandle` object corresponding to the current process

b. `isAlive()` – This returns a boolean value that indicates whether the process is alive or not

c. `pid()` – This returns the id of the process

d. `children()` – This returns a Stream of `ProcessHandle`

objects corresponding to the children of the current process.

279. In the code snippet below, explain what code should be used at line 1 to print the output in the expected output section below:

```
Optional<Double> price = <code here>; //Line 1
price.ifPresentOrElse(val -> System.out.println("Price
is not null"), () -> System.out.println("Price not
specified"));
```

Expected output:

```
Price not specified
```

Answer:

The code above uses the `ifPresentOrElse()` method added by Java 9 on the Optional class. This method accepts as parameter a `Consumer` instance and a `Runnable` instance. If a value is present in the Optional, it applies the `Consumer` on the value in the Optional. If a value is not present in the Optional, it executes the code specified on the Optional. In this case, we want the **Price Not Specified** output to be printed. The `Sysout` statement corresponding to this is specified in the `Runnable`. So, the Optional price must be an empty Optional in order for this code to be executed. So, Line 1 needs to be written as follows:

```
Optional<Double> price = Optional.empty();
```

280. What are the advantages of the new HttpClient introduced by Java 9?

Answer:

Java 9 has introduced a new `HttpClient` class that can be used to make an Http request through Java code. Prior to

Java 9, the `UrlConnection` and the `HttpUrlConnection` classes could be used to make an HTTP request. The new Java `HttpClient` has several advantages over these classes as follows:

a. The `HttpUrlConnection` only supports HTTP 1.1 which is a very old version of HTTP. `HttpClient` supports Http 2.0 which is the latest version of HTTP

b. Code written via the `HttpClient` is much cleaner compared to the code written via `HttpUrlConnection`

c. `HttpClient` supports asynchronous processing via `CompletableFutures`. So, it has a method called `sendAsync` that sends an HTTP request asynchronously. It returns a `CompletableFuture` which can be used to obtain the response once the request is completed.

Scenario Based Questions

281. Suppose you create a new thread by extending the Thread class and you invoke the start method multiple times. What do you think will happen?

Answer:

When you invoke the `start()` method the first time, a new Thread will be spawned and the code specified within the `run()` method will get executed in the body of the thread. However, on subsequent invocation of the start method, an `IllegalThreadStateException` will occur. This is because you cannot start the same thread more than once. Threads follow a life cycle and have certain states during the life–cycle. When a thread is created the first time, it is in the **NEW** state. After the `start()` method is invoked it enters the **RUNNABLE** state and once the run method completed, it enters the **TERMINATED** state. So, when you invoke the start method on a running thread, it is already in the **RUNNABLE** state. This causes the `IllegalThreadStateException`. If you want to execute the code in the thread again, you need to create a new Thread.

282. Suppose you have a method that returns an integer value. The code is present within a try/catch/finally. There is a return statement in the try, catch and finally blocks. The return statement in the try block returns 1, the return statement in the catch block returns –1 and the return statement in the finally block returns 0. If an exception occurs, which value will be returned?

Answer:

In the scenario described above, the return statement within the finally block will get executed so the value **0** will be returned. Since an exception occurs in the try block, the rest of the body of the try block is skipped. So, the return statement within the try bock is not executed. Since an exception occurs, the code within the catch block will get executed. However, since a finally block is present, the return statement within the catch block is also not executed. The code within the finally block gets executed and the return statement from the finally block gets executed. If the finally block was not present, the return statement from the catch block would have been executed.

283. Suppose you have a static method in the Base class. And suppose you have a method with the same name in the sub-class. And suppose you create a Base class object and assign it a reference of the sub-class object and invoke the static method. Is this valid? If so, which version of the static method gets invoked?

Answer:

The above scenario is perfectly valid and will not cause any error. When this code is executed, the static method in the base class gets invoked. Normally, when you define a variable of the super–class type and assign it a sub–class object and invoke an overridden method, the method defined in the sub–class gets invoked. This is because Java uses the object assigned and not the reference variable to determine the version of an overridden method to invoke. However, in the scenario described above, the methods in the super–class and sub–class are static. Static methods cannot be overridden. So, if you have a static method in the base class and a method with the same name in the sub–class, this would not be an example of overriding. Rather, this is known as method hiding. In such a scenario, the version of the method invoked is not determined by the type of object assigned to the reference variable but by the type of the reference variable. In this case, a base class reference variable is used. So, the static method in the base class gets invoked.

284. **Suppose you have a method in a base class that throws an ArrayIndexOutOfBoundsException. And suppose this method is overridden in the sub–class and declares that it throws a RuntimeException. What do you think will happen?**

Answer:

The scenario above states that a base class method throws an `ArrayIndexOutOfBoundsException` which is an unchecked exception. The sub–class method overrides this method and declares that it throws a `RuntimeException`. This situation is valid and will not cause any error. In method overriding, a sub–class method is not allowed to throw a checked exception that is new or broader than the exception declared in the super–class method. However, this rule does not apply to unchecked exceptions. So, a sub–class method is free to declare any unchecked exception and this will not cause any error. If the subclass method had declared the `java.lang.Exception` or any of its sub–classes in the throws clause, a compile time error would have occurred. This is because `java.lang.Exception` is a checked exception.

285. Suppose you have a List of objects. You want to send it as a parameter to a client application but want to ensure that the client application does not make changes to it. How can you achieve this?

Answer:

In order to ensure that a client application does not make changes to a List, you need to obtain a read–only copy of the List and return that copy to the client application. The Collections class has several utility methods that return a read only copy of a Collection. For example, it has a method called `Collections.unmodifiableList`. This method accepts a List as parameter and returns a List which is a read–only copy of the input List. Once a read only copy of a Collection is obtained via this method, any attempt to modify the List (like adding or removing data) will result in a `UnsupportedOperationException`. So, If the client application tries to modify this List, the exception will occur.

286. Suppose you are reading 10000 String values from the database. You need to create a concatenated String with these values. Which is the most efficient way to achieve this?

Answer:

There are several ways in which you can concatenate String values. The mostly commonly used method is to use the concatenation operator (+). However, this is not at all efficient in terms of performance and should be avoided when you have a large number of Strings. This is because the String class is immutable. So, using the + operator results in the creation of a large number of Strings. Java provides the StringBuffer class. This has a method called append that can be used to create concatenated Strings. This has better performance since it is a mutable class. There is also another class called StringBuilder which is very similar to StringBuffer. The only difference is that StringBuffer is synchronized while StringBuilder is not. So StringBuilder has a slightly better performance compared to StringBuffer. So, if synchronization is not an issue, you can use StringBuilder, otherwise you can use StringBuffer.

287. **Suppose you are developing an application that performs a lot of mathematical calculations involving very large decimal numbers. Which data type will you use for your variables given that precision is important?**

Answer:

Normally, programmers use float or double data types while dealing with decimal numbers. However, these data types have a downside. While dealing with very large or very small numbers, a loss of precision can occur with these data types leading to inaccurate results. So, using these data types in situations where precision is important is not a good idea. Java provides a class called `java.lang.BigDecimal`. This class overcomes the limitations of the float and double data types. It does not lose precision while dealing with large or small numbers and therefore provides exact results. It has methods corresponding to all the arithmetic operations like addition, subtraction, multiplication and division. In addition, it supports a lot of other operations as well. So, it can be used to perform all mathematical operations and provides precise results. The only downside of `BigDecimal` is performance. However, if precision is a priority over performance, then `BigDecimal` should be used.

288. Suppose you are working on a multi–threaded application. A new requirement comes in where you need to store key–value pairs. Which is the most appropriate Collection to be used in such a scenario?

Answer:

The `java.util.Map` interface supports storing data as key–value pairs. The mostly commonly used implementation of the Map interface is HashMap. However, the problem with HashMap is that is it not thread safe and so not appropriate to be used in a multi–threaded application. There is a utility method on the Collections class called `synchronisedMap()`. It accepts a Map as an input and returns a thread–safe map corresponding to the Map object passed in. So, such a synchronized map can be used in a multi–threaded environment. There is also another Map implementation called `ConcurrentHashMap`. This is a thread–safe implementation of the Map interface and so suitable for use in a multi–threaded environment. `ConcurrentHashMap` has a slightly better performance than a synchronized Map. A synchronized Map synchronizes the complete Map object, so even a read operation is not allowed while some other thread is using the Map. The `ConcurrentHashMap` on the other hand does not synchronize the whole map, so it allows read operations while some other thread is writing to the Map. So, while both synchronized Map and `ConcurrentHashMap` are suitable in a multi–threaded environment, `ConcurrentHashMap` should be used if performance is a consideration.

289. **Suppose you need to create some utility methods in your application. What is the best practice for creating such methods? Where would you place them?**

Answer:

Most of the time, developers place utility methods in a separate util class. However, you should try and place utility code in the class that it is related to. So, for example if you have a class called `Car` and you need to create a utility method called `createCar`, it can be a static method in the `Car` class itself rather than having a separate `CarUtil` class. However, there are often programming situations where you may need to club together some unrelated utility methods. In such a case, you can create a separate class and create static utility methods in this class. Starting Java 8, you can also have static methods in an interface. Static interface methods help to group together utility methods without having to create an object of a class.

290. **Suppose you have developed an interface called FileWriter as part of an API. It has a writeToCsv file method that writes the contents passed in to a CSV file. The API is implemented by different applications that provide an implementation for the FileWriter interface. Now, suppose you are required to add a new method to the interface called writeToExcel which writes the contents passed in to an excel file. How can you go about with this change with minimal impact to the users of your API?**

Answer:

In the scenario described above, it is required to add a new method to the `FileWriter` interface. Simply adding the method to the interface will cause compilation errors in all the existing classes that implement the interface and will require all the classes to provide an implementation for the `writeToExcel()` method. The best way to go about this is to add the `writeToExcel()` method as a default method in the `FileWriter` interface. Default methods are a new feature added by Java 8. They allow you to create methods with method bodies in an interface. Classes that implement the interface, do not need to provide an implementation for default methods. So, adding the `writeToExcel()` method as a default method in the `FileWriter` interface will not impact the classes that implement `FileWriter`. Default methods are added by Java 8. So, if you are using an earlier Java version, then this solution would not work. In that case, you can create a new version of the `FileWriter` interface (say `FileWriterEnhanced`) that extends the current `FileWriter` and add the `writeToExcel()` method in the `FileWriterEnhanced` interface. In this case, the existing code that implements the `FileWriter` interface will work as it is. Any code that needs the `writeToExcel()` method will need to implement the `FileWriterEnhanced` interface.

SECTION

04

CORE JAVA

JAVA 8

JAVA 9

HUMAN RESOURCE

Creativity

291. Where do you find ideas?

Answer:

Ideas can come from all places, and an interviewer wants to see that your ideas are just as varied. Mention multiple places that you gain ideas from, or settings in which you find yourself brainstorming. Additionally, elaborate on how you record ideas or expand upon them later.

As an example:

I am constantly taking notes on a notepad or in my phone throughout the day of things I would like to revisit later. I get ideas during work meetings, listening to my coworkers struggles and updates, take notes and research later how we can improve workflow. I will also get ideas via my network when they put out new innovative things they are pursuing in their workplace, I will see how I may be able to apply those innovations in my own company.

292. How do you achieve creativity in the workplace?

Answer:

It's important to show the interviewer that you're capable of being resourceful and innovative in the workplace, without stepping outside the lines of company values. Explain where ideas normally stem from for you (examples may include an exercise such as list-making or a mind map), and connect this to a particular task in your job that it would be helpful to be creative in.

As an example:

I was assigned to a safety and wellness taskforce. Most people were walking on their breaks anyway, just not together. I signed up for a three month hosted walking challenge in which people could still walk on their own on their breaks, however, they were encouraged to interact with their coworkers and engage in some healthy competition in tracking their progress. This ended up getting more people to get up and exercise while also building morale and a sense of teamwork.

293. How do you push others to create ideas?

Answer:

If you're in a supervisory position, this may be requiring employees to submit a particular number of ideas, or to complete regular idea-generating exercises, in order to work their creative muscles. However, you can also push others around you to create ideas simply by creating more of your own. Additionally, discuss with the interviewer the importance of questioning people as a way to inspire ideas and change.

As an example:

Each staff meeting I encourage staff members to bring a problem or challenge they have been facing or had faced since our last meeting, along with a solution. I also encourage employees to attend regular professional development opportunities whether it is a free webinar, a training, or even read newly published articles in their field, and share things they have learned or trending topics with the team.

294. Describe your creativity.

Answer:

Try to keep this answer within the professional realm, but if you have an impressive background in something creative outside of your employment history, don't be afraid to include it in your answer also. The best answers about creativity will relate problem-solving skills, goal-setting, and finding innovative ways to tackle a project or make a sale in the workplace. However, passions outside of the office are great, too (so long as they don't cut into your work time or mental space).

As an example:

I participate in a volunteer group outside of work who provides meals for homeless people. The company I worked for was seeking connections to the community and ways for the employees to be involved in something bigger than their specific roles at work, so with permission form the company, I hosted a fundraising event put on the company where the employees worked a spaghetti dinner to raise funds for the homeless charity. This boosted employee teamwork and comradery and a sense of purpose amongst them.

Leadership

295. Would you rather receive more authority or more responsibility at work?

Answer:

There are pros and cons to each of these options, and your interviewer will be more interested to see that you can provide a critical answer to the question. Receiving more authority may mean greater decision-making power and may be great for those with outstanding leadership skills, while greater responsibility may be a growth opportunity for those looking to advance steadily throughout their careers.

As an example:

I would say I am a good example of a "servant leader" in how I work within teams. I have a natural ability to lead and people naturally follow me. I am a natural project manager and can see the big picture as well as minute details. With that said, I listen to what my team says and encourage and value all of their input. It is all about having the ability to lead and make concise and proper decisions, while at the same time taking in to account the opinions and ideas of the entire team and allowing for improving in your decisions when need be.

296. What do you do when someone in a group isn't contributing their fair share?

Answer:

This is a particularly important question if you're interviewing for a position in a supervisory role - explain the ways in which you would identify the problem, and how you would go about pulling aside the individual to discuss their contributions. It's important to understand the process of creating a dialogue, so that you can communicate your expectations clearly to the individual, give them a chance to respond, and to make clear what needs to change. After this, create an action plan with the group member to ensure their contributions are on par with others in the group.

As an example:

I would say I am a good example of a "servant leader" in how I work within teams. I have a natural ability to lead and people naturally follow me. I am a natural project manager and can see the big picture as well as minute details. With that said, I listen to what my team says and encourage and value all of their input. It is all about having the ability to lead and make concise and proper decisions, while at the same time taking in to account the opinions and ideas of the entire team and allowing for improving in your decisions when need be.

297. Tell me about a time when you made a decision that was outside of your authority.

Answer:

While an answer to this question may portray you as being decisive and confident, it could also identify you to an employer as a potential problem employee. Instead, it may be best to slightly refocus the question into an example of a time that you took on additional responsibilities, and thus had to make decisions that were outside of your normal authority (but which had been granted to you in the specific instance). Discuss how the weight of the decision affected your decision-making process, and the outcomes of the situation.

As an example:

I had a customer call requesting to have their monthly payment that was already due, waived due to service they felt was subpar. The manager was the only one with the authority to make this decision and was out that day. The customer was very upset and ready to cancel services. I deferred the payment that was due that day and over-rode the automatic cancelation that was set to take place since the customer was behind on payments, and assured the manager was going to contact the customer the next day. When they were able to speak, the customer issue was resolved and they decided to continue our services.

298. Are you comfortable going to supervisors with disputes?

Answer:

If a problem arises, employers want to know that you will handle it in a timely and appropriate manner. Emphasize that you've rarely had disputes with supervisors in the past, but if a situation were to arise, you feel perfectly comfortable in discussing it with the person in question in order to find a resolution that is satisfactory to both parties.

As an example:

I went to my supervisor with some adjustments that needed to be made to a report they had me format and submit to the owner of the company. When I approached the supervisor about their errors they became immediately defensive in nature, until I assured them I just happened to notice the discrepancies in numbers and wanted to bring it to their attention so they could adjust it prior to it being submitted, so he and our department looked good. I assured him that I was looking out for the integrity of the work we produced and wanted to do my best to support him. He thanked me and the report was submitted without errors.

299. If you had been in charge at your last job, what would you have done differently?

Answer:

No matter how many ideas you have about how things could run better, or opinions on the management at your previous job, remain positive when answering this question. It's okay to show thoughtful reflection on how something could be handled in order to increase efficiency or improve sales but be sure to keep all of your suggestions focused on making things better, rather than talking about ways to eliminate waste or negativity.

As an example:

I would have focused on more cross training of the department staff so we would have been able to better assist each other during our own downtime, or in times of an influx of workload or emergency situations in a team member's role or position. This would have helped minimize confusion and back log, allowing for the entire department to be more up to speed and efficient.

300. Do you believe employers should praise or reward employees for a job well done?

Answer:

Recognition is always great after completing a difficult job, but there are many employers who may ask this question as a way to infer as to whether or not you'll be a high-maintenance worker. While you may appreciate rewards or praise, it's important to convey to the interviewer that you don't require accolades to be confident that you've done your job well. If you are interviewing for a supervisory position where you would be the one praising other employees, highlight the importance of praise in boosting team morale.

As an example:

I believe that each employee is different in the way they respond to praise and rewards and if they even desire it. Some may desire it greatly and work toward praise, and some don't like being in the spotlight. It is important to make sure employees are aware they are hired to do a job and are expected to complete their tasks. With that said, employees are human, and have stressful days, outside lives, and at times even just showing up to work and working hard deserves praise in itself. It is important to let employees know they are valued as humans supporting the organization and not just an employee number. Quarterly free employee luncheons for all staff with music and food, and recognition of someone who may have gone above and beyond in an extraordinary circumstance is a great way to keep morale and comradery up.

301. What do you believe is the most important quality a leader can have?

Answer:

There are many important skills for a leader to have in any business, and the most important component of this question is that you explain why the quality you choose to highlight is important. Try to choose a quality such as communication skills, or an ability to inspire people, and relate it to a specific instance in which you displayed the quality among a team of people.

As an example:

Communication is key in leadership. Having the ability to take in to consideration all aspects and every scenario before making a decision, but being able to be the one to ultimately make the decision whether it is going to be popular or not, is something a leader needs to be able to do. The important part is being able to really listen to your employees and hear their concerns out, letting them know you value their opinion, then explain to them why you made the decision that you did. Most times employees just want to feel heard. Having open lines of communication at all times is essential for maintaining trust amongst the staff. I made the decision to adjust our vacation request policy to reflect employees need to request vacation at least two weeks prior to their time off, which was met with much dismay. Once I explained the decision was based upon having overlapping days off, inadequate staffing, unfairness amongst coworkers, and loss of profits and it was going to be better for the company and the employees, they understood.

302. Tell me about a time when an unforeseen problem arose. How did you handle it?

Answer:

It's important that you are resourceful, and level-headed under pressure. An interviewer wants to see that you handle problems systematically, and that you can deal with change in an orderly process. Outline the situation clearly, including all solutions and results of the process you implemented.

As an example:

As the safety officer at my last employer, I had an important two o'clock meeting with department heads that had been on the calendar for a month and could not be moved due to the executive's busy schedules. At the same time, I had an urgent safety issue in the field I needed to run out to. I was split between the two issues so I had my intern take the presentation I had prepared to the meeting, explain the situation, and show the presentation to them anyway. He clarified things he could and took notes on their questions and items he was not equipped to address, and we scheduled a follow up conference call for the next day to go over the pending questions I was not there to answer. We were able to tie up loose ends on the follow up call and move forward with the project the next day. The executives understood the situation I was faced with and appreciated not having to put the project on hold.

303. Can you give me an example of a time when you were able to improve X objective at your previous job?

Answer:

It's important here to focus on an improvement you made that created tangible results for your company. Increasing efficiency is certainly a very important element in business, but employers are also looking for concrete results such as increased sales or cut expenses. Explain your process thoroughly, offering specific numbers and evidence wherever possible, particularly in outlining the results.

As an example:

I was able to successfully reduce the hold time by 4 minutes on each customer call and streamline the wait list process by suggesting a software in which all customer service reps had access to a monitor that showed all customer calls. The monitor displayed how many calls were active, pending, or on hold (and with which rep), and which line they were on. Reps could easily hang up a call, look at the board and see which line needed to be picked up next. This improved workflow for the customer service department, allowed for approximately 20 more customer resolutions per day, increased profits by 30% in terms of new orders that could now come in, and increased customer satisfaction and company ratings.

304. Tell me about a time when a supervisor did not provide specific enough direction on a project.

Answer:

While many employers want their employees to follow very specific guidelines without much decision-making power, it's important also to be able to pick up a project with vague direction and to perform self-sufficiently. Give examples of necessary questions that you asked and specify how you determined whether a question was something you needed to ask of a supervisor or whether it was something you could determine on your own.

As an example:

I had a large project already pending when my supervisor was about to leave for vacation. Before her vacation she gave me another project and did not leave deadlines along with it. I analyzed the project and determined it was a new client and I did not want to leave them wondering. I continued with my pending project and made contact with the new client to introduce myself and set up a call to discuss their needs. This bought me time while also allowing me to obtain more information. It was still unclear as to what the deadlines were and it did not seem urgent so I continued with my existing, as well as set aside time each afternoon to begin working on the new client's project as well.

305. Tell me about a time when you were in charge of leading a project.

Answer:

Lead the interviewer through the process of the project, just as you would have with any of your team members. Explain the goal of the project, the necessary steps, and how you delegated tasks to your team. Include the results, and what you learned as a result of the leadership opportunity.

As an example:

As an HR Assistant helping while the HR Benefits Rep was out on leave, I was put in charge of the annual employee benefits open enrollment for a large organization. I spoke with the manager ahead of time to gather as much information as I could on what had worked in the past in terms of timelines and work flow, and added a couple of helpful changes myself such as a filing system for the different benefit changes as they were going to come in. The week prior to the beginning of open enrollment, I had a meeting with the HR department to go over each form and explain to my team how I was going to distribute each form and made helpful cheat sheets of information for them to each keep at their desk in instances of an employee coming with questions and I may be unavailable. The entire process went smoothly and organized, and employees commented on how easy it was.

306. Tell me about a suggestion you made to a former employer that was later implemented.

Answer:

Employers want to see that you're interested in improving your company and doing your part - offer a specific example of something you did to create a positive change in your previous job. Explain how you thought of the idea, how your supervisors received it, and what other employees thought was the idea was put into place.

As an example:

I suggested we start an innovation committee to bring staff together to discuss new ideas they had for the workplace. These ideas included a wide variety of things such as ways to implement employee recognition, snack machine options, changes to the customer lobby, and anything and everything in between. While not all ideas were acted upon by management, a variation of most of the ideas were implemented. This made the employees feel a sense of ownership and belonging in the company, as well as improved morale and teamwork.

307. Tell me about a time when you thought of a way something in the workplace could be done more efficiently.

Answer:

Focus on the positive aspects of your idea. It's important not to portray your old company or boss negatively, so doesn't elaborate on how inefficient a particular system was. Rather, explain a situation in which you saw an opportunity to increase productivity or to streamline a process, and explain in a general step-by-step how you implemented a better system.

As an example:

Our department had set aside Fridays as "filing days" for paperwork that was collected throughout the week. While this was definitely a great idea, if a coworker called out sick, or we had a large amount of filing in one week, there would be times when we would not get it all done on Friday, or it would be very stressful due to the high volume of paperwork we received throughout the week. I suggested that we started to file throughout the week during ourdowntime between projects so we would not have a backlog all on one day. I also noticed that the last half hour of each day, some coworkers would start "packing up" and with the work we did, we couldn't really start a new project within the last little bit of time so we would start packing up and then file for the last thirty minutes of each day until it was time to clock out. This greatly reduced the amount we had piled up for Fridays, as well as kept productivity higher throughout the week.

308. Is there a difference between leading and managing people - which is your greater strength?

Answer:

There is a difference - leaders are often great idea people, passionate, charismatic, and with the ability to organize and inspire others, while managers are those who ensure a system runs, facilitate its operations, make authoritative decisions, and who take great responsibility for all aspects from overall success to the finest decisions. Consider which of these is most applicable to the position, and explain how you fit into this role, offering concrete examples of your past experience.

As an example:

I am a good leader because I take time to think about all possible aspects of a project and how it may affect each employee tasked to work on the project. I do my best to see things from each perspective, anticipating and planning things that may go wrong, and focusing on what could go right. I pitch ideas in a way where I am able to garner support from the employees and make them feel they are a part of something great.

309. Do you function better in a leadership role, or as a worker on a team?

Answer:

It is important to consider what qualities the interviewer is looking for in your position, and to express how you embody this role. If you're a leader, highlight your great ideas, drive and passion, and ability to incite others around you to action. If you work great in teams, focus on your dedication to the task at hand, your cooperation and communication skills, and your ability to keep things running smoothly.

As an example:

While I am able to work well in either role, I find that I am better suited for leadership roles since it comes so naturally for me. Even in positions where I was not the boss, I had people coming to me for suggestions, to bounce ideas off of, and looking for support. I am good at project management and fitting the right people in to the right place where their skills and personality, as well as work ethic will be best suited. If I find someone on a team is struggling with keeping up, I am able to find creative ways to include them and change their tasks to something possibly even outside of their comfort zone, where they are better suited to contribute to the team. I find the best quality in each employee and motivate them in to action.

310. **Tell me about a time when you discovered something in the workplace that was disrupting your (or others) productivity - what did you do about it.**

Answer:

Try to not focus on negative aspects of your previous job too much, but instead choose an instance in which you found a positive, and quick, solution to increase productivity. Focus on the way you noticed the opportunity, how you presented a solution to your supervisor, and then how the change was implemented (most importantly, talk about how you led the change initiative). This is a great opportunity for you to display your problem-solving skills, as well as your resourceful nature and leadership skills.

As an example:

Our one and only timeclock was continuously met with long lines of all staff clocking out at the same time. This would cause chaos at the clock out line, disgruntled employees, employees in a hurry skipping the process entirely, and employees packing up for the day early so they could "get in line." I suggested we add a second timeclock on the other side of the room near the second entry door to alleviate the line. This helped productivity because employees did not feel the need to pack up early and waste time standing at a timeclock and eased some of the grumpiness felt at the end of the day.

311. **How do you perform in a job with clearly-defined objectives and goals?**

Answer:

It is important to consider the position when answering this question - clearly, it is best if you can excel in a job with clearly-defined objectives and goals (particularly if you're in an entry level or sales position). However, if you're applying for a position with a leadership role or creative aspect to it, be sure to focus on the ways that you additionally enjoy the challenges of developing and implementing your own ideas.

As an example:

I enjoy having a set guideline of rules to abide by. This helps to streamline processes, especially when dealing in customer-centric companies. With that said, if I see a policy that can be improved on, I have no problem with bringing my ideas to the forefront, testing them and if they work, implementing them. With the improvement in a process, the policy would need to be updated, and all employees notified of the new procedures so all staff are on the same page.

312. How do you perform in a job where you have great decisionmaking power?

Answer:

The interviewer wants to know that, if hired, you won't be the type of employee who needs constant supervision or who asks for advice, authority, or feedback every step of the way. Explain that you work well in a decisive, productive environment, and that you look forward to taking initiative in your position.

As an example:

I have been given the opportunity to be in the role of decision maker many times in previous roles. There are times where a guideline exists of how to properly perform the job and limitations within your role, however, there are instances where you must make a prompt decision on the spot. During these times I have no problem with being creative in solving a problem and informing my superiors of what took place afterward, to keep them in the loop.

313. If you saw another employee doing something dishonest or unethical, what would you do?

Answer:

In the case of witnessing another employee doing something dishonest, it is always best to act in accordance with company policies for such a situation - and if you don't know what this company's specific policies are, feel free to simply state that you would handle it according to the policy and by reporting it to the appropriate persons in charge. If you are aware of the company's policies (such as if you are seeking a promotion within your own company), it is best to specifically outline your actions according to the policy.

As an example:

This really depends on what they were doing. Some things such as stealing large amounts of money, equipment, or anything that puts themselves or someone else in danger, would need to be reported immediately. There may be times however, where a coworker is perhaps breaking a policy or going around protocol to save time or cut costs, and it may be detrimental to themselves or the company. In these instances, I would feel comfortable discussing the issue with my coworker myself and seeing if I can help them in any way and let them know that what they were doing was wrong. They may not have even realized it was wrong or may have been going through rough times. If they continued to do so even after we spoke, I would feel comfortable bringing the issue to management.

314. Tell me about a time when you learned something on your own that later helped in your professional life.

Answer:

This question is important because it allows the interviewer to gain insight into your dedication to learning and advancement.

Choose an example solely from your personal life, and provide a brief anecdote ending in the lesson you learned. Then, explain in a clear and thorough manner how this lesson has translated into a usable skill or practice in your position.

As an example:

I work with a volunteer organization on the weekends. When the president of the organization was unavailable to lead a fundraising event, I had to step in and assure the event went smoothly, set it up, and emcee to the crowd. I was very nervous but this ended up helping increase my public speaking skills drastically, and the next team meeting we had at work I was able to speak to my coworkers and present my project without feeling nervous. I also was asked to coordinate the next employee event at work and used some of the things from the volunteer event I worked at in the employee event at work, such as seating arrangement and check in process. I became a more valued member of the team at work.

315. Tell me about a time when you developed a project idea at work.

Answer:

Choose a project idea that you developed that was typical of projects you might complete in the new position. Outline where your idea came from, the type of research you did to ensure its success and relevancy, steps that were included in the project, and the end results. Offer specific before and after statistics, to show its success.

As an example:

We were having difficulties in hiring new sales staff. I developed the idea to update our sales position job descriptions. The job descriptions we had were outdated and had not been updated in several years, during which time, many new software tools had become available, and the position had changed. The sales team got together and reviewed the current job description and provided their input as to what they felt should be added and removed from the descriptions, then management reviewed and made updates accordingly. Once we began running job ads with the new job description, we had an increase in qualified sales professionals applying who understood the position they applied for and were better matches.

316. Tell me about a time when you took a risk on a project.

Answer:

Whether the risk involved something as complex as taking on a major project with limited resources or time, or simply volunteering for a task that was outside your field of experience, show that you are willing to stretch out of your comfort zone and to try new things. Offer specific examples of why something you did was risky and explain what you learned in the process - or how this prepared you for a job objective you later faced in your career.

As an example:

I worked in the engineering department of a utility company. We had an emergency situation where a water pipe broke in the community and were overwhelmed with customer calls from the community regarding their utility bills. During this time, there were two customer service reps out on leave, so I offered my assistance since I was in between major projects. I was completely out of my comfort zone however I assisted with taking customer calls, answering basic questions, and taking names and numbers of the customers I was unable to help, so the supervisor could call them back later. I was able to collect payment from approximately 100 customers, successfully answer about 50 questions, and take information for call backs on another 25. I learned more about how what I did in my department connected to the customer service reps and the types of questions they are asked by customers and challenges they face.After this situation, our two departments began working together more, and even had quarterly meetings together where we provided updates on items that may directly impact the work of the other department.

317. What would you tell someone who was looking to get into this field?

Answer:

This question allows you to be the expert - and will show the interviewer that you have the knowledge and experience to go along with any training and education on your resume. Offer your knowledge as advice of unexpected things that someone entering the field may encounter and be sure to end with positive advice such as the passion or dedication to the work that is required to truly succeed.

As an example:

If someone were looking to get into the field of sales, I would suggest first looking in to what certificate programs or degree options are available that may help with the field. I would also suggest if you are not comfortable with speaking to others whether one on one or in group settings, to take a public speaking class to boost your confidence. I would suggest learning the ins and outs about sales and finding a product that you are truly passionate about selling. If you are not passionate about your business, especially in sales, you will not do well. Once you find what you are passionate about selling, learn everything you can about it. If it is a product, use itand test it. If it is a service, try it out. Remember to allow yourself time in the beginning to fail a few times, this is not the end of the world as it helps you learn. Keep being persistent in your work and learn what works and does not work with your target audience. Have a positive attitude with customers and clients, find a balance between seeming too pushy or eager, but not too timid and disinterested, and don't forget the follow ups after making first contact!

Deadlines and Time Management

318. Tell me about a time when you didn't meet a deadline.

Answer:

Ideally, this hasn't happened - but if it has, make sure you use a minor example to illustrate the situation, emphasize how long ago it happened, and be sure that you did as much as you could to ensure that the deadline was met. Additionally, be sure to include what you learned about managing time better or prioritizing tasks in order to meet all future deadlines.

As an example:

I rarely, if ever miss a deadline. With that said, I do recall about two years ago I missed a deadline in submitting a report to the finance department. The problem ended up being that I had taken on too many projects all at once, and then had a couple of "urgent" unexpected issues thrown in as well that same week. I failed to ask for help, thinking I could do it all on my own and not wanting to give my supervisor the impression that I couldn't handle the job. What happened though was that I did let the supervisor down and when I sat down to discuss the issue with them they assured me that if I had just kept the communication open about my workload, they would have helped pick up the slack. From then on, I made sure to be more open with my supervisor with my current workload and express any concerns I have with deadlines. I have not missed a deadline since, and my relationship with my team mates and productivity within the department have both improved along with the more open communication.

319. How do you eliminate distractions while working?

Answer:

With the increase of technology and the ease of communication, new distractions arise every day. Your interviewer will want to see that you are still able to focus on work, and that your productivity has not been affected, by an example showing a routine you employ in order to stay on task.

As an example:

Each morning, I look over the days tasks and prepare for what I need to do. I check my e-mail, messages, and other personal items and then put away my personal devices. I make sure my family and friends know that I check messages only during breaks, and that if there is an emergency they have a good phone number to reach me. During breaks during the work week, I do not engage in a lot of social media, as that can drag in to the work day. On my breaks I prefer to walk, read, check in with a coworker for a few minute chat, or message a family or friend to say hello then it is back to work.

320. **Tell me about a time when you worked in a position with a weekly or monthly quota to meet. How often were you successful?**

Answer:

Your numbers will speak for themselves, and you must answer this question honestly. If you were regularly met your quotas, be sure to highlight this in a confident manner and don't be shy in pointing out your strengths in this area. If your statistics are less than stellar, try to point out trends in which they increased toward the end of your employment, and show reflection as to ways you can improve in the future.

As an example:

I consistently meet my deadlines every quarter. I take what the company gives me as a quota then I add my own personal goal to that. This way, I have something higher to work toward, and allows wiggle room if I am able to meet just the company goal and not my own as well. I try not to focus too much on the daily sales but rather do a monthly check. This allows for me to not spend too much wasted time on worrying about progress while still making sure I am on target.

321. **Tell me about a time when you met a tough deadline, and how you were able to complete it.**

Answer:

Explain how you were able to prioritize tasks, or to delegate portions of an assignments to other team members, in order to deal with a tough deadline. It may be beneficial to specify why the deadline was tough - make sure it's clear that it was not a result of procrastination on your part. Finally, explain how you were able to successfully meet the deadline, and what it took to get there in the end.

As an example:

I was placed with the large task of submitting a state report I had never done before, due to my coworkers sudden absence. I researched the topic on my own downtime when I could, reached out to other companies to see how they were completing the project, and I found an online training I could take during business hours. With permission from my boss, I delegated my clerical duties to the department secretary until I was able to finish the state report. I was able to submit it ahead of schedule and it added value to my job and me as an employee, as I was asked to assist with other projects after that, received a great performance review and raise during subsequent evaluation period.

322. How do you stay organized when you have multiple projects on your plate?

Answer:

The interviewer will be looking to see that you can manage your time and work well - and being able to handle multiple projects at once, and still giving each the attention it deserves, is a great mark of a worker's competence and efficiency. Go through a typical process of goal-setting and prioritizing, and explain the steps of these to the interviewer, so he or she can see how well you manage time.

As an example:

I keep an ongoing list of tasks on a notepad and Outlook calendar. Each morning when I arrive to work, I look at my Outlook calendar and I review the written list of tasks that I had added the day before on a notepad throughout the day, and prioritize what needs to be done that day and what can wait. For the tasks that can be done later in the week, I utilize the calendar feature in Outlook to put tasks on specific dates, so a reminder pops up prompting me to complete the task. Of the items on the list that can not wait, I choose the quickest and complete those first. Then I dive in to the more complex tasks. During the day when urgent items arise that put me off my schedule, I revisit my Outlook calendar and written list and constantly adjust accordingly. I also keep in communication with my team mates and let them know if there are any items I could use assistance with if they have downtime.

323. How much time during your workday do you spend on "auto-pilot?"

Answer:

While you may wonder if the employer is looking to see how efficient you are with this question (for example, so good at your job that you don't have to think about it), but in almost every case, the employer wants to see that you're constantly thinking, analyzing, and processing what's going on in the workplace. Even if things are running smoothly, there's usually an opportunity somewhere to make things more efficient or to increase sales or productivity. Stress your dedication to ongoing development and convey that being on "auto-pilot" is not conducive to that type of success.

As an example:

I am very good at my job and do find myself going in to "auto-pilot" often. With that said, when I complete a project or task, I take time to review the completed project to assure accuracy. If I get the project done with downtime to spare after, I may try to test out a different method of completion to see if there are ways to improve the process. Sometimes there is and sometimes there simply isn't, however, I constantly find ways to utilize my time in the most effective and proficient manner.

324. How do you handle deadlines?

Answer:

The most important part of handling tough deadlines is to prioritize tasks and set goals for completion, as well as to delegate or eliminate unnecessary work. Lead the interviewer through a general scenario and display your competency through your ability to organize and set priorities, and most importantly, remain calm.

As an example:

I utilize my Outlook calendar for ongoing tasks that I know have to be completed on a recurring basis. For example, every Monday I have to submit my sales report, and every Wednesday I have to file. If there are any special projects coming up that I need to prepare for, I will set aside time and reminders on my calendar to prepare for the upcoming project. I also take time every morning when I get to work to review the tasks I have that day, and do the same at the end of each day as well to be sure I completed everything I needed to and prepare for the next day. If I feel that I am unable to meet a deadline for some reason, I communicate this with the department I am working with and see if any adjustments need to be made. Communication is key. Additionally, I am constantly mindful of the need to adjust my schedule accordingly if urgent projects arise.

325. Tell me about your personal problem-solving process.

Answer:

Your personal problem-solving process should include outlining the problem, coming up with possible ways to fix the problem, and setting a clear action plan that leads to resolution. Keep your answer brief and organized, and explain the steps in a concise, calm manner that shows you are level-headed even under stress.

As an example:

When I was working as an equipment mechanic, I began experiencing difficulty in managing the amount of work coming in from multiple project managers in my company. Each of them started pairing me as the technician over their client's equipment. I tried to tell some of them no, and I was told I was not a team player. I ended up discussing with the shop foreman what the issue was and explained I was a team player but simply did not have enough time in the day to finish all of the jobs they were giving me. I started a scheduling board in my work area where I put what jobs I had, who the project manager was, what phase I was in with each project, and expected completion time. This allowed for all project managers to clearly see my workload, and better understand and appreciate the work I was doing, while allowing them to figure out if they wanted to pursue someone else to repair their client's equipment or wait for me to have an opening.

326. What sort of things at work can make you stressed?

Answer:

As it's best to stay away from negatives, keep this answer brief and simple. While answering that nothing at work makes you stressed will not be very believable to the interviewer, keep your answer to one generic principle such as when members of a team don't keep their commitments, and then focus on a solution you generally employ to tackle that stress, such as having weekly status meetings or intermittent deadlines along the course of a project.

As an example:

When someone I work with is not pulling their weight, it can be stressful if it ends up affecting my job negatively. During these times I remain calm and talk it out with the team. I offer assistance when I can and work on ways to better the situation. I do my best to maintain a positive and pleasant attitude, since acting out negatively will do nothing but make the situation worse. I was working on a project with three coworkers. We each had specific tasks that all tied into each other's tasks. If one of us fell behind, we all fell behind. One co-worker was consistently behind the rest of us and the entire project was falling behind. I pulled the coworker aside and asked them if they needed assistance and explained to them that their lackof promptness was making the rest of us fall behind. I had the conversation in a very non-accusatory manner and kept things light. I offered helpful suggestions on ways they can improve their timeliness and then suggested we have daily morning meetings as a team to see where each of us was at. This allowed for more transparency amongst the team and opened a door for conversations on ways for that coworker to improve, which ended up helping us complete the project on time.

327. How do you outwardly respond to stress in the workplace? How do you calm yourself down when you are feeling stressed?

Answer:

This is a trick question - your interviewer wants to hear that you don't look any different when you're stressed, and that you don't allow negative emotions to interfere with your productivity. As far as how you solve your stress, it's best if you have a simple solution mastered, such as simply taking deep breaths and counting to 10 to bring yourself back to the task at hand.

As an example:

When I begin to feel stressed about a situation at work, I sometimes tend to get very quiet and take too long to think of the right response

I want to give or message I want to relay to the team. In these instances, I know that it is important to let the team know that while I am feeling a little stressed at the moment, I willbe ok and am just thinking of the proper way to handle the situation. I make sure to take a deep breath, maintain composure, smile and say I am going to take a quick break. I remove myself from the situation and step outside, or even sit for a moment in the breakroom and read a book. If staff ask me what I am doing I just simply tell them lightheartedly I needed a moment to think of how I am going to awesomely respond to the situation, or if it is a more serious topic or situation I may say I just needed a moment to recharge. Then I regroup and rejoin my team.

328. Are you good at multi-tasking? Give some examples of how you successfully multi-tastk?

Answer:

Some people can, and some people can't. The most important part of multi-tasking is to keep a clear head at all times about what needs to be done, and what priority each task falls under. Explain how you evaluate tasks to determine priority, and how you manage your time in order to ensure that all are completed efficiently.

As an example:

I am a good multi-tasker because I am able to respond to changes quickly. I keep running lists of what I am working on so if I have interruptions or urgent projects that take me away from my existing tasks, I am able to quickly go back to what I was working on.

329. How many hours per week do you work?

Answer:

Many people get tricked by this question, thinking that answering more hours is better - however, this may cause an employer to wonder why you have to work so many hours in order to get the work done that other people can do in a shorter amount of time. Give a fair estimate of hours that it should take you to complete a job and explain that you are also willing to work extra whenever needed.

As an example:

If I am working a full time forty-hour work week job, then that is what I work. Lets be honest we are human… so there have been times where I was not feeling well so I was slow, or having some off weeks where I may have only worked thirty eight hours or so, however, I did not miss any deadlines and as soon as I was feeling better I was back at my usual work speed and productivity hours. On the other hand, if I feel I need to work any overtime I will only do so if I have permission from the supervisor first. There was one instance when I had an emergency arise and it was time for me to leave, however if I left, then it would have made things worse for the company and the client, so I did stay an extra thirty minutes to complete the task, however I immediately called my supervisor of the issue and why I stayed, so they were aware.

330. How many times per day do you check your email?

Answer:

While an employer wants to see that you are plugged into modern technology, it is also important that the number of times you check your email per day is relatively low - perhaps two to three times per day (dependent on the specific field you're in). Checking email is often a great distraction in the workplace, and while it is important to remain connected, much correspondence can simply be handled together in the morning and afternoon.

As an example:

I check my e-mail about three or four times a day. Typically, when I arrive to the office, before and after lunch, and before I leave for the day. There may be instances when things are slow in the office and I check less, or there may be times when I am waiting on an e-mail containing information I need to start a certain task, or I am in communication with a customer back and forth about an important topic, so I may check or respond more frequently. On an average day though, no more than about four times per day.

Customer Service

04

331. What is customer service?

Answer:

Customer service can be many things - and the most important consideration in this question is that you have a creative answer. Demonstrate your ability to think outside the box by offering a confident answer that goes past a basic definition, and that shows you have truly considered your own individual view of what it means to take care of your customers. The thoughtful consideration you hold for customers will speak for itself.

As an example:

Customer Service is basically any interaction you have with other people during the course of a work day. If you are working in customer service it's simple – you answer the phone, take payments, solve problems. If you work in HR, your customers may be the employees you serve. If you work in sales, your customers may be the people you sell to. Customer Service is show you work with others, your attitude, and your problem-solving abilities. It is wanting to always provide the best service possible, in any capacity you can, to whomever you encounter while at work.

332. Tell me about a time when you went out of your way for a customer.

Answer:

It's important that you offer an example of a time you truly went out of your way - be careful not to confuse something that felt like a big effort on your part, with something your employer would expect you to do anyway. Offer an example of the customer's problems, what you did to solve it, and the way the customer responded after you took care of the situation.

As an example:

I was working with a new client on a large construction job. The client was ready to go with their job and then fell on financial hardship. I wanted to be sure to help the client out so I worked out a payment plan where they did not have to pay for it all upfront. I had them sign a contract noting that I adjusted the payment plan and that it was a one-time situation so they were aware if they used us again in the future it may be payment up front again. The new client was appreciative and the project was completed. We were able to maintain a long-standing relationship with the client and ended up getting more work from them down the road as well as good reviews and increased visibility within the community as a result of word spreading.

333. How do you gain confidence from customers?

Answer:

This is a very open-ended question that allows you to show your customer service skills to the interviewer. There are many possible answers, and it is best to choose something that you've had great experience with, such as "by handling situations with transparency," "offering rewards," or "focusing on great communication." Offer specific examples of successes you've had.

As an example:

Open communication is always good in gaining customer confidence. Instead of just giving any answer just for the sake of providing an answer, I am sure to let the customer know if I don't have an immediate answer to their question and assure them that I will get the right answer and get back with them. Then, I make sure to follow through. Without communication and follow through you will lose trust and they will take their business elsewhere. The customer appreciates honesty and the time you take in delivering them the right answer and the best service.

334. Tell me about a time when a customer was upset or agitated - how did you handle the situation?

Answer:

Similarly, to handling a dispute with another employee, the most important part to answering this question is to first set up the scenario, offer a step-by-step guide to your particular conflict resolution style, and end by describing the way the conflict was resolved. Be sure that in answering questions about your own conflict resolution style, that you emphasize the importance of open communication and understanding from both parties, as well as a willingness to reach a compromise or other solution.

As an example:

Customers who are upset just want to be heard. It is important to listen. I had a customer call when I worked in a billing call center, complaining that she felt she was being charged too much on her monthly bill. She was already agitated when she called and I quickly realized that the more I tried to talk, the more upset she got. I took the time to listen and allow her to fully explain the situation. It became apparent to me that she had not been keeping up to date with the notices that were sent out explaining that there were rate increases. I informed her of the rate increase and waived the first month rate increase, then sent her the notices via e-mail for her to review. I called her the next day to follow up and see if she had any questions.

335. When can you make an exception for a customer?

Answer:

Exceptions for customers can generally be made when in accordance with company policy or when directed by a supervisor. Display an understanding of the types of situations in which an exception should be considered, such as when a customer has endured a particular hardship, had a complication with an order, or at a request.

As an example:

Typically, there are protocols and policies in place to assure that operations are running smoothly and that all customers are being treated fairly while still making sure the company is profitable and not being taken advantage of. There may be times when a customer has an unusual or unexpected hardship that makes it difficult for them to keep up on their payments, and in these situations an extension should be given as a one time courtesy. If the issue continues into the next month, I review the policy manual to see if there is anything else that can be offered and if not, I go to the supervisor for assistance and guidance. At that point it is typically up to the supervisor to make the next call.

336. What would you do in a situation where you were needed by both a customer and your boss?

Answer:

While both your customer and your boss have different needs of you and are very important to your success as a worker, it is always best to try to attend to your customer first - however, the key is explaining to your boss why you are needed urgently by the customer, and then to assure your boss that you will attend to his or her needs as soon as possible (unless it's absolutely an urgent matter).

As an example:

The customer always comes first, and bosses know this most of the time. In situations where a boss may request your assistance at the same time as a customer, it's easy to approach the boss to see what it is they need, get the information, and explain to them that you will be jumping on that task as soon as you are finished assisting the customer. The customer is your source of business and you need to be sure they are taken care of in a timely manner.

337. What is the most important aspect of customer service?

Answer:

While many people would simply state that customer satisfaction is the most important aspect of customer service, it's important to be able to elaborate on other important techniques in customer service situations. Explain why customer service is such a key part of business and be sure to expand on the aspect that you deem to be the most important in a way that is reasoned and well-thought out.

As an example:

The most important aspect of customer service is being genuine. If you do not have a product that genuinely helps the customer, or you are not genuine in your delivery of customer service, the company will fail. Having the ability to enjoy delivering the best customer service and being excited about helping the customer makes the customer also feel excited to do business with you and they feel confident they are being taken care of. Having a pleasant attitude sets the tone for any conversation with a customer and being sure to follow throughand do your job to the best of your ability makes the customer feel confident in your services.

338. Is it best to create low or high expectations for a customer?

Answer:

You may answer this question either way (after, of course, determining that the company does not have a clear opinion on the matter). However, no matter which way you answer the question, you must display a thorough thought process, and very clear reasoning for the option you chose. Offer pros and cons of each and include the ultimate point that tips the scale in favor of your chosen answer.

As an example:

It's good to create high expectations from the beginning of any relationship with a newcustomer. This shows you have confidence and makes the customer excited to be on the journey with you. While creating such high expectations though,you should be sure to communicate realistic processes and timeframes so the customer knows that while you are their best choice and they will be glad they chose your company, that things don't happen overnight and a certain level of patience and understanding will need to be had by the customer while they wait for their product to be delivered. Be sure to let them know the wait will be worth it, because you are the best! High expectations, creating excitement, and open communication so they know what to expect, are all important.

Communication

339. Describe a time when you communicated a difficult or complicated idea to a co-worker.

Answer:

Start by explaining the idea briefly to the interviewer, and then give an overview of why it was necessary to break it down further to the coworker. Finally, explain the idea in succinct steps, so the interviewer can see your communication abilities and skill in simplification.

As an example:

I had the idea of a new job scheduling system and needed to present it to the team. I had limited resources and we had not obtained the necessary software yet, so what I did was type up a brief overview of the idea and add main bullet points with images and screen shots of the software from the internet and compiled it into a PowerPoint presentation. I attempted to think of all potential questions that may come up during the meeting and different perspectives so I would be ready to answer questions and present it in a way that would appeal to everyone. I included a list of pros and cons, to include solutions to each con that may come up as well so the team understood I had thought out and was well prepared.

340. What situations do you find it difficult to communicate in?

Answer:

Even great communicators will often find particular situations that are more difficult to communicate effectively in, so don't be afraid to answer this question honestly. Be sure to explain why the particular situation you name is difficult for you and try to choose an uncommon answer such as language barrier or in time of hardship, rather than a situation such as speaking to someone of higher authority.

As an example:

It can sometimes be difficult to communicate effectively when delivering bad news. It is easy to become stressed, or worried about how the person will react. It is important to not attempt to communicate until you feel prepared. Be ready to listen instead of just talk, answer questions you have the answers to, and offer a sense of empathy for what the person is thinking or feeling. Above all it's important to communicate openly and confidently, so the person feels comfortable and has confidence in you or the situation.

341. What are the key components of good communication?

Answer:

Some of the components of good communication include an environment that is free from distractions, feedback from the listener, and revision or clarification from the speaker when necessary. Refer to basic communication models where necessary and offer to go through a role-play sample with the interviewer in order to show your skills.

As an example:

I find it best to be sure to make eye contact and avoid distractions such as the phone or computer while having a serious conversation. Knowing it's ok to ask for clarification is important so there are not any instances of misunderstandings. Reflective listening is a great tool in any communication, where you show the person you were listening to them by repeating back certain things they said when appropriate (For example "I hear you saying you need more support with this project. Let's work on how we can fix it and get you the support you need.

342. Tell me about a time when you solved a problem through communication.

Answer:

Solving problems through communication is key in the business world, so choose a specific situation from your previous job in which you navigated a messy situation by communicating effectively through the conflict. Explain the basis of the situation, as well as the communication steps you took, and end with a discussion of why communicating through the problem was so important to its resolution.

As an example:

My department was having too many misunderstandings due to lack of in person communication and only speaking through e-mail. We never checked our e-mail at the same time and were never on the same page. We continued to overlap on work and tasks were not evenly distributed, with many tasks falling through the cracks. Additionally, there were instances where directives were not clear via e-mail. I requested our department make time for at least bi-weekly department meetings to make sure we were all on the same page and allow time without distraction to address each other and provide updates on department projects. This time together built comradery among the team and provided an effective way to open more lines of communication.

343. Tell me about a time when you had a dispute with another employee. How did you resolve the situation?

Answer:

Make sure to use a specific instance, and explain step-by-step the scenario, what you did to handle it, and how it was finally resolved. The middle step, how you handled the dispute, is clearly the most definitive - describe the types of communication you used, and how you used compromise to reach a decision. Conflict resolution is an important skill for any employee to have and is one that interviewers will search for to determine both how likely you are to be involved in disputes, and how likely they are to be forced to become involved in the dispute if one arises.

As an example:

When I had a dispute with a coworker I asked if we could talk about the issue. They clearly were not interested at first. I let them have their space and checked back a couple of days later, while gently pushing the fact that I respected them and wanted to put the issue behind us so we can both move forward and work together better. I proposed a few different times to meet to discuss the issue and allowed them to choose the time that worked best for them. This made them feel as though they were in some position of control and had buy in. Once we met, I explained again I wanted to move forward and focused on the positive traits about them and our team working

abilities and asked them how they felt we should resolve the issue.
I listened intently and offered my input once they were finished.
We moved forward and put it behind us after that and were able to
effectively communicate better than ever before We were also more
comfortable to approach each other with any other issues that arose
from then on out.

344. Do you build relationships quickly with people, or take more time to get to know them?

Answer:

Either of these options can display good qualities, so determine which style is more applicable to you. Emphasize the steps you take in relationship-building over the particular style and summarize briefly why this works best for you.

As an example:

I feel I get along with anyone pretty quickly and easily build effective
working relationships. I am always careful to not get too comfortable
too fast, as certain aspects of any relationship take time to develop.
While I may run in to people throughout the course of my career that
I just do not mesh with well, I am still able to maintain a professional
working relationship and mutual respect with them.

345. Describe a time when you had to work through office politics to solve a problem.

Answer:

Try to focus on the positives in this question, so that you can use the situation to your advantage. Don't portray your previous employer negatively, and instead use a minimal instance (such as paperwork or a single individual), to highlight how you worked through a specific instance

resourcefully. Give examples of communication skills or
problem-solving you used in order to achieve a resolution.

As an example:

There have been many times where I needed to work my way
through the "red tape" that was a part of office procedures in getting
approvals for new work permits. Although at times it was very
frustrating and time consuming, I understood this was necessary as
it took time to review the plans and assure the job was going to be
done according to safety and legal protocols. I had a job that needed
to be rushed, so I prepared a letter explaining the situation, had a
statement from the business owner who the job was for, and had my
supervisor contact the signing authority to present my case. I was
sure to include reasons why the project would affect the community
negatively if put on hold or if it took too long to build, and how
rushing the job would be good for the community and opening that
store would have a trickle effect in opening other stores in the same
vacant lot. While the job ended up not being done the next day, it
was moved up two weeks ahead of the original schedule.

346. Tell me about a time when you persuaded others to take on a difficult task.

Answer:

This question is an opportunity to highlight both your
leadership and communication skills. While the specific
situation itself is important to offer as background, focus on
how you were able to persuade the others, and what tactics
worked the best.

As an example:

I had a coworker who was reluctant to help me implement a new
filing system. The project was going to be time consuming and
difficult. I presented her key points on how the project would benefit

*herself and the entire department and make her job easier, and told
her that ultimately it would be something the boss would look kindly
on and an opportunity for her to shine. I motivated her by telling her
she had really great ideas and that if she were a part of the project it
would help for it to get done faster and more efficiently because of
her knowledge and ideas. Making her feel good about herself and feel
needed motivated her to help.*

**347. Tell me about a time when you successfully persuaded a
group to accept your proposal.**

Answer:

This question is designed to determine your resourcefulness
and your communication skills. Explain the ways in which you
took into account different perspectives within the group and
created a presentation that would be appealing and convincing
to all members. Additionally, you can pump up the proposal
itself by offering details about it that show how well-executed
it was.

As an example:

*I was trying to purchase a new invoice software that no one was
interested in but me. The reason they were not interested was
because they were comfortable in the current software and felt they
were too busy to learn a new system. I researched the software I was
interested in, put together a bullet point list and handed it out to
each department member ahead of a scheduled meeting so they would
have time to look at it and bring questions with them, and then
showcased the software to the team using screen shots and in depth
information on how the software would make their jobs easier. I took
a couple of coworkers jobs specifically and pointed out how it would
directly impact their jobs and improve their processes. I allowed
them time to think about it and do more research on their own before*

making a decision.

348. Tell me about a time when you had a problem with another person, that, in hindsight, you wished you had handled differently.

Answer:

The key to this question is to show your capabilities of reflection and your learning process. Explain the situation, how you handled it at the time, what the outcome of the situation was, and finally, how you would handle it now. Most importantly, tell the interviewer why you would handle it differently now - did your previous solution create stress on the relationship with the other person, or do you wish that you had stood up more for what you wanted? While you shouldn't elaborate on how poorly you handled the situation before, the most important thing is to show that you've grown and reached a deeper level of understanding as a result of the conflict.

As an example:

Many years ago, I had a coworker who never wanted to listen to anything I said, or any of my ideas. They were very stuck in their ways and reluctant in learning new things. I thought the best thing to do was to just avoid them and let them do their own thing and avoid confrontation. In hindsight I could have done better to understand their perspective and potentially their fear of change, and make better attempts at communicating the need for a new process and assuring them that the new process may have made their job easier and we were all a team and would support each other throughout any change. Over the years my ability to communicate and realize that communication is important for teamwork and ultimately the company, has dramatically improved.

349. Tell me about a time when you negotiated a conflict between other employees.

Answer:

An especially important question for those interviewing for a supervisory role - begin with a specific situation and explain how you communicated effectively to each individual. For example, did you introduce a compromise? Did you make an executive decision? Or, did you perform as a mediator and encourage the employees to reach a conclusion on their own?

As an example:

I had many instances as shop supervisor when I acted as a mediator in a dispute between two employees. There was not one go-to solution that would work for every situation since each employee was different and each situation or dispute was different. I would carefully reflect upon the dispute and make a determination for what needed to be done based off of the facts that I was aware of and the personalities of the involved parties. Most often, having both employees sit down together to discuss with me acting as a witness and mediator was very effective. I made sure to allow each the opportunity to present what happened, their perspective, and then how it made them feel or what they thought the best outcome would be. I was sure to always point out that both could have handled the situation differently to avoid the dispute escalating and pointed out the positive traits about each that I felt would allow them to move forward and work together better. I was always sure to follow up to make sure things were still going smoothly and I always had an open door policy if they ran into issues again.

Job Searching and Scheduling

350. What are the three most important things you're looking for in a position?

Answer:

The top three things you want in a position should be similar to the top three things the employer wants from an employee, so that it is clear that you are well-matched to the job. For example, the employer wants a candidate who is well-qualified for and has practical experience - and you want a position that allows you to use your education and skills to their best applications. The employer wants a candidate who is willing to take on new challenges and develop new systems to increase sales or productivity - and you want a position that pushes you and offers opportunities to develop, create, and lead new initiatives. The employer wants a candidate who will grow into and stay with the company for a long time - and you want a position that offers stability and believes in building a strong team. Research what the employer is looking for beforehand and match your objectives to theirs.

As an example:

The three things I am looking for would be opportunity to apply my skillset to make a positive impact, opportunity for growth and learning new things, and stability in a company with a positive mission.

351. How are you evaluating the companies you're looking to work with?

Answer:

While you may feel uncomfortable exerting your own requirements during the interview, the employer wants to see that you are thinking critically about the companies you're applying with, just as they are critically looking at you. Don't be afraid to specify what your needs from a company are (but do try to make sure they match up well with the company - preferably before you apply there) and show confidence and decisiveness in your answer. The interviewer wants to know that you're the kind of person who knows what they want, and how to get it.

As an example:

I am looking at employee satisfaction, company stability, and type of service the company offers. I want to be sure that I am working at a company with good employee feedback so I know the company takes good care of the people on the front lines making the company succeed. I also want to know the company will be around a while and I can stay and grow with the company. Finally, if I want to work with a company that offers a good service to the community and I feel passionate about going to work each day.

352. Are you comfortable working for _____ salary?

Answer:

If the answer to this question is no, it may be a bit of a deal-breaker in a first interview, as you are unlikely to have much room to negotiate. You can try to leverage a bit by highlighting specific experience you have, and how that makes you qualified for more, but be aware that this is very difficult to navigate at this step of the process. To avoid this situation, be aware of industry standards and, if possible, company standards, prior to your application.

As an example:

I am definitely comfortable with starting out at that pay rate. I am happy for the opportunity and know that I will continue to grow within the company.

353. Why did you choose your last job?

Answer:

In learning what led you to your last job, the interviewer is able to get a feel for the types of things that motivate you. Keep these professionally-focused and remain passionate about the early points of your career, and how excited you were to get started in the field.

As an example:

I chose my last job because it was at a non-profit. The pay was lower than a privately held company, however, I knew that it would be a good experience and they needed the help. My skills and knowledge were a great addition to their company and at the time I was able to live off the pay that I received. It was a great experience and now that time has gone by I am ready to move forward in my career and take it to the next level whether it be in non-profit or not, I would like to be able to elevate my career.

354. How long has it been since your last job and why?

Answer:

Be sure to have an explanation prepared for all gaps in employment, and make sure it's a professional reason. Don't mention difficulties you may have had in finding a job, and instead focus on positive things such as pursuing outside interests or perhaps returning to school for additional education.

As an example:

I held my last job about a year ago. I had a very demanding job with long hours, and was doing well financially, however I took some time off for rest and focus on more family time that I felt I was missing out on. During that time, I took some professional development courses and also re-focused my goals and am ready to get back in to the workforce. I feel refreshed, re-trained and re-focused on the area of my field that I am most interested in pursuing.

355. What other types of jobs have you been looking for?

Answer:

The answer to this question can show the interviewer that you're both on the market and in demand. Mention jobs you've applied for or looked at that are closely related to your field, or similar to the position you're interviewing for. Don't bring up last-ditch efforts that found you applying for a part-time job completely unrelated to your field.

As an example:

Because I am pursuing a marketing career, I am focused on

marketing jobs in public sector. I am applying mostly for marketing assistant positions and may also be interested in administrative roles if I am still able to have a hand at marketing. I feel pretty confident in my abilities as a successful marketing assistant so I am doing my best to get my foot in the door in that arena, where I can help a company expand their horizons with new creative marketing strategies.

356. Have you ever been disciplined at work?

Answer:

Hopefully the answer here is no - but if you have been disciplined for something at work though, be absolutely sure that you can explain it thoroughly. Detail what you learned from the situation and reflect on how you grew after the process.

As an example:

I have not been disciplined at work however I did receive some criticism on keeping my supervisor better informed on my progress during major projects. I had a tendency to be in the zone and push forward at my own rate, and get the job done and did not think at the time it was important to keep my supervisor up to date if nothing was going wrong. I thought that if something was going wrong, that would be the time to get my boss involved. After discussion, I learned that the supervisor actually had reports they had to submit to upper management once a week, and they had to include my project and where I was at in the process. Once I learned that, I realized that keeping my boss up to date on my projects, even when everything was going right, was always important.

357. What is your availability like?

Answer:

Your availability should obviously be as open as possible, and any gaps in availability should be explained and accounted for. Avoid asking about vacation or personal days (as well as other benefits) and convey to the interviewer how serious you are about your work.

As an example:

I reviewed the business hours and believe my availability would match what the job requires. While I obviously need time to tend to family and personal matters, I am also willing to work overtime as needed as well in order to support the organization.

358. May I contact your current employer?

Answer:

If possible, it is best to allow an interviewer to contact your current employer as a reference. However, if it's important that your employer is not contacted, explain your reason tactfully, such as you just started job searching and you haven't had the opportunity yet to inform them that you are looking for other employment. Be careful of this reasoning though, as employers may wonder if you'll start shopping for something better while employed with them as well.

As an example:

I don't mind at all if you contact my current employer. I would prefer if you were to wait until a contingent offer is made and allow me time to speak with my employer first, out of respect for them so they are not blind sided though. While they were aware that I may eventually leave to grow my career, they will be understandably immediately concerned with filling my position since I play such an important part of the organization. I'd like to be able to speak with them first before they receive a phone call.

359. Do you have any valuable contacts you could bring to our business?

Answer:

It's great if you can bring knowledge, references, or other contacts that your new employer may be able to network with. However, be sure that you aren't offering up any of your previous employer's clients, or in any way violating contractual agreements.

As an example:

I do have some great contacts at other agencies who work with the same software I work with in the accounting field. We have been able to troubleshoot and problem solve together over the years and they share great new ideas with me that help me with things that come up. I'd definitely have much support. I also have a few people who are business owners that can share with your management team any insight they have with how to handle employee issues and new business trends.

360. How soon would you be available to start working?

Answer:

While you want to be sure that you're available to start as soon as possible if the company is interested in hiring you, if you still have another job, be sure to give them at least two weeks' notice. Though your new employer may be anxious for you to start, they will want to hire a worker whom they can respect for giving adequate notice, so that they won't have to worry if you'll eventually leave them in the lurch.

As an example:

While I am eager and excited to begin working with you, I would prefer to give a two week notice to my current employer, out of respect. This will allow time for tying up loose ends and allow me to help them transition during and after my departure.

361. Why would your last employer say that you left?

Answer:

The key to this question is that your employer's answer must be the same as your own answer about why you left. For instance, if you've told your employer that you left to find a position with greater opportunities for career advancement, your employer had better not say that you were let go for missing too many days of work. Honesty is key in your job application process.

As an example:

I believe my last employer would say I left for growth opportunities. While they were sad to see me go, I know they were happy with the time I spent there, and I appreciate of the knowledge I gained while working there.

362. How long have you been actively looking for a job?

Answer:

It's best if you haven't been actively looking for a job for very long, as a long period of time may make the interviewer wonder why no one else has hired you. If it has been awhile, make sure to explain why, and keep it positive. Perhaps you haven't come across many opportunities that provide you with enough of a challenge or that are adequately matched to someone of your education and experience.

As an example:

I haven't actually been looking for a specific amount of time. I typically only look at job ads if someone sends me something they feel I'd be good at or interested in, as I was not in a hurry to leave my last employer. I saw this job ad and was excited about it so applied for it. It seems like a great opportunity and I feel I would be a good fit. I couldn't pass up on the opportunity to interview and the chance to further my career with your company.

363. When don't you show up to work?

Answer:

Clearly, the only time acceptable to miss work is for a real emergency or when you're truly sick - so don't start bringing up times now that you plan to miss work due to vacations or family birthdays. Alternatively, you can tell the interviewer how dedicated to your work you are, and how you always strive to be fully present and to put in the same amount of work every time you come in, even when you're feeling slightly under the weather.

As an example:

Typically, it takes a lot for me to miss work. I will go to work if I have the sniffles I am not one to call in sick because I sneezed or have a slight headache. At the same time, I do not want to get anyone else sick so if I feel truly under the weather, I am sure to stay home. Additionally, of course if there were to be a family emergency that would warrant a sick day, I would give my supervisor ample notice as soon as I found out the need for it. I am good at keeping my boss informed. I also let the boss know of any urgent tasks that may need to be addressed should I expect to miss an entire day so nothing falls too far behind and there is complete transparency.

364. Have you ever been told by your supervisor to leave work for the day? If so, why?

Answer:

The response to this question will most likely be no, however, if there ever was an instance you were sent home for the day whether it be because you were too sick for work, were having a bad day or being insubordinate, try to word it in a way where you project you understood the reason and have since worked on improving.

As an example:

I have only been sent home once and that was when I was very sick for almost a week. I missed two days of work and was falling behind on my workload. I felt good enough to go to work on the third day and didn't want to fall farther behind. I didn't a fever and felt good enough to show up so I did, but within a couple of hours immediately felt drained, tired, and it was clear that I was not as well as I thought. The boss had asked me when I got there if I was sure I was ok to be at work and I said yes. A couple of hours later she ended up telling me to just go home since it was becoming increasingly difficult to focus with the congestion and weakness I was feeling. I went home and was glad I did. I slept and returned the next day. Nowadays I am better at being sure to take care of myself first and be sure I am good enough to go to work, since health comes first.

365. What is your attendance record like?

Answer:

Be sure to answer this question honestly, but ideally you will have already put in the work to back up the fact that you rarely miss days or arrive late. However, if there are gaps in your attendance, explain them briefly with appropriate reasons, and make sure to emphasize your dedication to your work, and reliability.

As an example:

> *My attendance record is pretty good. I can't say I have perfect attendance because I am human and have gotten sick enough a couple of times where I needed to call in sick, or had certain appointments that were only available during the same hours I worked. Other than that, I am consistent in showing up to work every day and on time. During rare occurrences of running a few minutes late, I made sure to all and let my boss know, and then even made up for it during lunch or end of day with the bosses' permission.*

366. Where did you hear about this position?

Answer:

This may seem like a simple question, but the answer can actually speak volumes about you. If you were referred by a friend or another employee who works for the company, this is a great chance to mention your connection (if the person is in good standing!). However, if you heard about it from somewhere like a career fair or a work placement agency, you may want to focus on how pleased you were to come across such a wonderful opportunity.

As an example:

> *I heard about the position when a friend of mine sent it to me. She thought it looked interesting and had heard good things about the company. I don't typically care too much about job ads however when I read this one I was excited and very interested and didn't want to pass up the opportunity to apply.*

367. Tell me anything else you'd like me to know when making a hiring decision.

Answer:

This is a great opportunity for you to give a final sell of yourself to the interviewer - use this time to remind the interviewer of why you are qualified for the position, and what you can bring to the company that no one else can. Express your excitement for the opportunity to work with a company pursuing X mission.

As an example:

If you hire me you will not be disappointed. I am excited at the opportunity and eager to be able to help your company grow. My skillset and experience seem to match the position perfectly. I'm excited at the prospect of joining the team and seeing how I can "bring solutions to the community" like your company mission says!

Index

Core Java Interview Questions

OOPs Concepts

001. Explain method overloading and method overriding

002. Explain the benefits of OOPs.

003. Write a code snippet that demonstrates encapsulation.

004. What are the types of inheritance relationships?

005. What is the best practice in declaring instance variables?

006. What is a singleton class?

007. Explain what happens when the following code is compiled and state whether it uses method overloading or overriding.

008. Write a Java code sample that demonstrates method overloading

009. What is polymorphism? How does Java support Polymorphism?

010. Explain how Java achieves abstraction

Java Basics

011. What are the possible ways of declaring the Java main method?

012. What are the possible ways of declaring a Java class?

013. How will you define an Identifier?

014. What are the modifiers that cannot be specified with an instance variable?

015. What are the modifiers that can be specified with a method declaration?

016. What will be the default value of a reference variable when it is not explicitly initialized? How will you handle this in code?

017. Explain the keywords "transient" and "native"

018. What is a comment in Java? Explain the types of comments supported by Java

019. Explain what is JVM, JRE and JDK

020. Explain with a code sample how you will read a value entered by a user

Data Types, Variables and Arrays

021. What are the possible ways of declaring an array of short data type?

022. How will you cast an int variable to byte explicitly? Is it really necessary to cast int literal to byte?

023. Give an example of implicit casting.

024. Write a code snippet that demonstrate how you can assign a float value to a short variable

025. What is the default value for int, double, float, boolean, long and char data types?

026. In the following code snippet, explain which lines will compile fine and which will cause a compilation error

027. Explain what happens when the following code is compiled

028. You are given an assignment to create a game of Tic Tac Toe using a multi–dimensional array. Which of the following is the correct way to initialize the array?

029. Explain the primitive data types in Java

030. What are the possible ways to assign a decimal number to a float variable?

031. Identify the error in the following code snippet and explain how it can be fixed

032. How will you assign an Octal and Hexadecimal literal to an "int" variable?

033. In the code snippet below, which lines will compile and which will cause an error?

034. What happens when the following code is compiled and executed?

035. Consider the following code snippet and explain its output

Operators

036. In the code snippet below, which lines will cause a compilation error and why?

037. What will be the output of the following code and why?

Control Statements

061. What happens when you compile and execute the code below? What will be the output?

062. Give some examples of "for–each" loop

063. What will be the output of the following code?

064. What will happen when you execute the code below? If it compiles fine, what will be the output?

Classes and Methods

065. Consider the following code snippet:

    What will be the output when this code is compiled and executed?

066. Can an instance variable be declared as static? Explain.

067. Explain what happens when the following code is compiled and executed.

068. What happens behind the scenes if a constructor is not explicitly specified?

069. Explain what happens when the following code is compiled

070. What are the possible access specifiers for a constructor?

071. What will be the output of the following code snippet?

072. How will you define a constructor? Give an example.

073. Explain the void keyword with a code sample

074. Explain the differences between a constructor and an ordinary method

075. Explain this keyword with a code sample

076. Explain the differences between a class and an object

077. Explain the new keyword with a code sample

078. What will be the output of the following code snippet?

079. Explain the return keyword with a code sample

Inner Classes

080. What is an inner class? What are the different types of inner classes?

081. Write a code sample that demonstrates how you can instantiate an inner class from an outer class

105. Can a class implement two interfaces? What will happen if both the interfaces have a method with the same name?

106. What is the use of abstract classes?

107. Explain what is the issue with the following code snippet:

108. Is the following code snippet valid? Explain the reasons either ways

109. Which lines in the following code will cause a compilation error?

110. Is the code snippet below valid? Explain

Packages and Access Control

111. What is a package? What are the advantages of packages?

112. Explain the Java access specifiers.

113. Explain with a code sample how to create a package

114. Name some default packages in JDK and explain what they do in brief

115. Is the following code valid? Explain the reasons

116. Explain the import keyword

117. Explain the differences between the protected and default access specifier

118. Is the following code snippet valid? Explain

119. Explain what happens when the following code is compiled and executed:

120. Explain the java.lang package

Exception Handling

121. Explain 'throw', 'throws' and 'Throwable' in Java.

122. What will be the output when you compile and execute the following code?

123. Write a code sample that demonstrates the try/catch/finally block:

124. What will be the output on executing the code below?

125. Explain the try–catch–finally statement in Java.

126. What will be the output of the following code snippet?

127. Suppose you have a method called myMethod with some code that can throw a checked Exception. How will you handle this in the code?

128. What is the use of "finally" clause? Give an example.

129. Explain the differences between Error and Exception

130. What is a RuntimeException?

String Handling

131. What is a string literal? Give an example..

132. What will be the output of the following code? Explain why

133. What will be the output when the following code is executed?

134. What will be the output of the following code snippet?

135. What are the various ways of assigning a string literal to a String variable?

136. Name some commonly used methods from the String class

137. What is the difference between StringBuffer and StringBuilder?

138. Write a code sample that reverses a String without using a loop.

139. Write a code sample that demonstrates how you can convert a String to uppercase.

140. Explain how you can convert an Integer to a String

Generics

141. What happens when you compile and run the following code?

142. Will Line 1 in the following line of code compile? If not, state the reasons.

143. Explain the issue with the following code.

144. Explain what additional code is required to make the code snippet below valid:

145. Explain Bounded Generic Types with a code sample

Collections

146. What are the four main interfaces in the Java Collection API

147. How will you search for a specific element in an array?

148. Which collection would you choose if do not want duplicates and do not care about the order?

149. Explain with a code sample how you can remove the head of a queue

150. Which collection implementation allows growing or shrinking its size and provides indexed access to its elements?

151. Explain the Queue interface.

152. Explain the Comparator interface

153. Explain some of the methods on the Queue Interface

154. Is it possible to mix generic and non–generic collections? If so, give example.

155. What are some of the important methods on the Collection interface?

Enumerations, Autoboxing and Wrapper Classes

156. What are the wrapper classes available in Java?

157. What will be the output of the following code?

158. Explain how you will convert a String "100.55" to a Double and a Double 100.55 to a String

159. What will be the output the following code?

160. What is a Wrapper class in Java? What are the special properties of Wrapper class objects?

161. Explain Autoboxing with an example

Threads

162. How will you create Threads in Java?

163. Explain the different types of Threads in Java

164. Can the run method be invoked directly without invoking the start method?

165. What happens behind the scenes when the following code is executed?

166. Explain some of the main methods in the Thread class

167. Explain thread states

168. Write a code sample that creates a thread using the "Thread" class.

169. Write a code sample that creates a thread using the Runnable interface.

170. Is it possible to create more than one thread in a Java application? If so, how will the threads communicate with each other?

171. What is Synchronization?

172. Explain what happens when the following code is executed

173. Consider the following code:

Executing this code first prints "Thread 1" 1000 times and then prints the "Thread 2" 1000 times. If this is incorrect, explain the reasons.

174. Write a code sample that makes a thread pause for ten minutes

175. What happens when a synchronized method is invoked?

Java IO API

176. What happens when the following code is executed?

177. Write a code sample that creates a file in the path /usr/test.txt.

178. Explain the FileWriter class with a code sample

179. Write a code snippet that reads the content in the file /usr/CoreJava. txt using a FileReader and displays the output in the console.

180. Explain with a code sample how you can create a directory on the file system.

181. Explain what happens when the following code is compiled and executed

182. Write a code sample that demonstrates the PrintWriter class.

183. Write a code sample that demonstrates how to delete a file

184. Write a code sample that demonstrates how to rename a file or directory.

185. Which classes are used to serialize and de-serialize objects?

186. Explain some of the important methods on the File class

Miscellaneous

187. Explain what happens when the following code snippet is compiled

188. Explain what happens when the following code is compiled and executed

189. Explain symmetric equals() contract.

190. Which of the following are invalid statements and why?

191. What is the use of transient keyword?

192. What is Garbage Collection in Java?

193. Which part of the memory is used in Garbage Collection? Which algorithm does the JVM use for Garbage collection?

194. When does garbage collection occur?

195. What code needs to be written in order to trigger garbage collection?

196. Explain with a code sample how an object becomes eligible for garbage collection.

Functional Interfaces

197. What is a functional interface? How can you create a functional interface?

198. Explain the java.util.Function package

199. Explain the java.util.function.Consumer interface with a code sample

200. Explain the differences between the Supplier and Consumer interfaces.

201. What is the output of the following code snippet?.

202. Which in–built functional interface would you use to convert a String to uppercase?

203. Is the code below valid? Explain.

204. Name some pre–Java 8 interfaces that are made functional interfaces by Java 8

205. Why are primitive specializations of the in–built functional interfaces like IntSupplier, BooleanSupplier, etc. added by Java 8?

206. Where are the built–in functional interfaces commonly used?

Lambda Expressions

207. What is a lambda expression? What are the benefits of using lambda expressions?

208. How are lambda expressions and functional interfaces related to each other?

209. Explain the syntax of a lambda expression

210. Give some examples of lambda expressions

211. Write a code sample that creates a Functional interface and use a Lambda expression to implement it

212. Explain with a code sample how the same functional interface can be implemented differently using different lambda expressions

213. Identify the error in the following lambda expression and how it can be fixed

214. Is the following code valid? Explain

215. Write a functional interface for which the following lambda expression would work

216. Explain how you can create a new Thread using lambda expression.

Streams

217. Explain the different ways in which you can create a Stream.

218. Explain the Stream filter operation with a code sample.

219. Explain the types of Stream operations.

220. What is a parallel stream? Explain with a code sample how you can create a parallel stream.

221. How can you convert a Stream back to a Collection?

222. What is the output of the following code snippet?

223. What is the difference between a Stream and a Collection?

224. Suppose you have a List of String values. You want to create a new List that eliminates the duplicates from the original List and has the String values in uppercase. How will you achieve this via Stream operations?

225. Is it possible to convert an array to a Stream? Explain

226. Suppose you have an Employee class as follows:

     And suppose you have a List of Employee objects as follows:
     How can you create a new List is sorted based on the Employee salary using Streams?

Method References

227. What is a method reference? What are the benefits of method references?

228. What are the different types of method references?

229. Give an example of static method reference.

230. Consider the following Shape class:

     What changes are required in this class in order to make the code below valid?

231. Explain what type of method reference is String::toUpperCase

DateTime API

232. Explain what is wrong in the following code snippet and how you can fix it

233. Explain with appropriate code samples the different ways in which you can create a LocalDate

234. Explain with a code sample how you can check if a date is before another date

235. Explain the ZonedDateTime class

236. What will be the output of the following code snippet?

237. How can you obtain the day of the week corresponding to a date using the Java 8 DateTime API?

238. Explain the differences between the Period and Duration class

239. Suppose you have a String date in the yyyy/mm/dd format. How can you obtain a LocalDate object corresponding to such a date?

240. What is the output of the following code snippet?

241. Explain how you can find out if a year is a leap year using the new DateTime API

Static and Default Interface Methods

242. What are static and default methods? Why were they introduced by Java 8?

243. What is the difference between an abstract class and an interface after Java 8?

244. Write a code sample that demonstrates a default method

245. What is the difference between a static and a default interface method?

246. Identify the error in the following code snippet and explain how it can be fixed

Optionals

247. What is an Optional and why was it added by Java 8?

248. How can an Optional be created?

249. Explain the Optional.ifPresent method with a code sample

250. What is the difference between the orElse and orElseThrow method?

251. What will be the output of the following code snippet?

Collection Improvements

252. Explain with a code sample how the forEach method works

253. What are some of the improvements made by Java 8 on the List interface?

254. How does the Map.getOrDefault method work?

255. What is the output of the following code snippet?

256. Explain the differences between an Iterator and SplitIterator

Miscellaneous

257. What are the advantages of CompletableFuture class over the Future Interface?

258. What is StringJoiner? Explain with a code sample

259. Explain the differences between the Comparator.reverse and Comparator.reverseOrder methods

260. dentify the error in the code below and explain what needs to be done to fix it

261. Explain the differences between the CompletableFuture.runAsync and the CompletableFuture.supplyAsync methods

Modules

262. What is a module? What benefits do they offer?

263. What is the module descriptor?

264. What is the difference between a package and a module?

265. Explain the changes made to JDK for Java 9

266. Consider the following code snippet:

     In order for this code to be deployed as part of a module, what needs to be done?

267. Explain the requires static module directive. When should it be used?

Stream/Collection Improvements

268. What are some of the improvements made by Java 9 on the Stream Interface?

269. Is the code below valid? If not, what can be done to fix it?

270. Identify the issue in the code snippet below and explain how it can be fixed

271. Which Java 9 method can you use to create a Set of String values?

272. What will be the output of the following code snippet?

Miscellaneous

273. What changes are made by Java 9 to interfaces and why?

274. What is JShell?

275. What is the output of the following code snippet?

276. What changes has Java 9 made to the try–with statement?

277. What is the use of the stream method added by Java 9 on the Optional class?

278. Explain the ProcessHandle class and some of its important methods

279. In the code snippet below, explain what code should be used at line 1 to print the output in the expected output section below:

Expected output:

280. What are the advantages of the new HttpClient introduced by Java 9?

Scenario Based Questions

281. Suppose you create a new thread by extending the Thread class and you invoke the start method multiple times. What do you think will happen?

282. Suppose you have a method that returns an integer value. The code is present within a try/catch/finally. There is a return statement in the try, catch and finally blocks. The return statement in the try block returns 1, the return statement in the catch block returns –1 and the return statement in the finally block returns 0. If an exception occurs, which value will be returned?

283. Suppose you have a static method in the Base class. And suppose you have a method with the same name in the sub–class. And suppose you create a Base class object and assign it a reference of the sub–class object and invoke the static method. Is this valid? If so, which version of the static method gets invoked?

284. Suppose you have a method in a base class that throws an ArrayIndexOutOfBoundsException. And suppose this method is overridden in the sub–class and declares that it throws a RuntimeException. What do you think will happen?

285. Suppose you have a List of objects. You want to send it as a parameter to a client application but want to ensure that the client application does not make changes to it. How can you achieve this?

286. Suppose you are reading 10000 String values from the database. You need to create a concatenated String with these values. Which is the most efficient way to achieve this?

287. Suppose you are developing an application that performs a lot of mathematical calculations involving very large decimal numbers. Which data type will you use for your variables given that precision is important?

288. Suppose you are working on a multi–threaded application. A new requirement comes in where you need to store key–value pairs. Which is the most appropriate Collection to be used in such a scenario?

289. Suppose you need to create some utility methods in your application. What is the best practice for creating such methods? Where would you place them?

290. Suppose you have developed an interface called FileWriter as part of an API. It has a writeToCsv file method that writes the contents passed in to a CSV file. The API is implemented by different applications that provide an implementation for the FileWriter interface. Now, suppose you are required to add a new method to the interface called writeToExcel which writes the contents passed in to an excel file. How can you go about with this change with minimal impact to the users of your API?

Creativity

291. Where do you find ideas?

292. How do you achieve creativity in the workplace?

293. How do you push others to create ideas?

294. Describe your creativity.

Leadership

295. Would you rather receive more authority or more responsibility at work?

296. What do you do when someone in a group isn't contributing their fair share?

297. Tell me about a time when you made a decision that was outside of your authority.

298. Are you comfortable going to supervisors with disputes?

299. If you had been in charge at your last job, what would you have done differently?

300. Do you believe employers should praise or reward employees for a job well done?

301. What do you believe is the most important quality a leader can have?

302. Tell me about a time when an unforeseen problem arose. How did you handle it?

303. Can you give me an example of a time when you were able to improve X objective at your previous job?

304. Tell me about a time when a supervisor did not provide specific enough direction on a project.

305. Tell me about a time when you were in charge of leading a project.

306. Tell me about a suggestion you made to a former employer that was later implemented.

307. Tell me about a time when you thought of a way something in the workplace could be done more efficiently.

308. Is there a difference between leading and managing people – which is your greater strength?

309. Do you function better in a leadership role, or as a worker on a team?

310. Tell me about a time when you discovered something in the workplace that was disrupting your (or others) productivity – what did you do about it?

311. How do you perform in a job with clearly-defined objectives and goals?

312. How do you perform in a job where you have great decision-making power?

313. If you saw another employee doing something dishonest or unethical, what would you do?

314. Tell me about a time when you learned something on your own that later helped in your professional life.

315. Tell me about a time when you developed a project idea at work.

316. Tell me about a time when you took a risk on a project.

317. What would you tell someone who was looking to get into this field?

Deadlines and Time Management

318. Tell me about a time when you didn't meet a deadline.

319. How do you eliminate distractions while working?

320. Tell me about a time when you worked in a position with a weekly

or monthly quota to meet. How often were you successful?

321. Tell me about a time when you met a tough deadline, and how you were able to complete it.

322. How do you stay organized when you have multiple projects on your plate?

323. How much time during your work day do you spend on "auto-pilot?"

324. How do you handle deadlines?

325. Tell me about your personal problem-solving process.

326. What sort of things at work can make you stressed?

327. How do you outwardly respond to stress in the workplace? How do you calm yourself down when you are feeling stressed?

328. Are you good at multi-tasking? Give some examples of how you successfully multi-task?

329. How many hours per week do you work?

330. How many times per day do you check your email?

Customer Service

331. What is customer service?

332. Tell me about a time when you went out of your way for a customer.

333. How do you gain confidence from customers?

334. Tell me about a time when a customer was upset or agitated – how did you handle the situation?

335. When can you make an exception for a customer?

336. What would you do in a situation where you were needed by both a customer and your boss?

337. What is the most important aspect of customer service?

338. Is it best to create low or high expectations for a customer?

Communication

339. Describe a time when you communicated a difficult or complicated idea to a coworker.

340. What situations do you find it difficult to communicate in?

341. What are the key components of good communication?

342. Tell me about a time when you solved a problem through communication.

343. Tell me about a time when you had a dispute with another employee. How did you resolve the situation?

344. Do you build relationships quickly with people, or take more time to get to know them?

345. Describe a time when you had to work through office politics to solve a problem.

346. Tell me about a time when you persuaded others to take on a difficult task.

347. Tell me about a time when you successfully persuaded a group to accept your proposal.

348. Tell me about a time when you had a problem with another person, that, in hindsight, you wished you had handled differently.

349. Tell me about a time when you negotiated a conflict between other employees.

Job Searching and Scheduling

350. What are the three most important things you're looking for in a position?

351. How are you evaluating the companies you're looking to work with?

352. Are you comfortable working for _____ salary?

353. Why did you choose your last job?

354. How long has it been since your last job and why?

355. What other types of jobs have you been looking for?

356. Have you ever been disciplined at work?

357. What is your availability like?

358. May I contact your current employer?

359. Do you have any valuable contacts you could bring to our business?

360. How soon would you be available to start working?

361. Why would your last employer say that you left?

362. How long have you been actively looking for a job?

363. When don't you show up to work?

364. Have you ever been told by your supervisor to leave work for the day? If so, why?

365. What is your attendance record like?

366. Where did you hear about this position?

367. Tell me anything else you'd like me to know when making a hiring decision.

Some of the following titles might also be handy

1. NET Interview Questions You'll Most Likely Be Asked
2. Access VBA Programming Interview Questions You'll Most Likely Be Asked
3. Administrator & Helpdesk Interview Questions You'll Most Likely Be Asked
4. Adobe ColdFusion Interview Questions You'll Most Likely Be Asked
5. Advanced C++ Interview Questions You'll Most Likely Be Asked
6. Advanced Excel Interview Questions You'll Most Likely Be Asked
7. Advanced JAVA Interview Questions You'll Most Likely Be Asked
8. Advanced SAS Interview Questions You'll Most Likely Be Asked
9. AJAX Interview Questions You'll Most Likely Be Asked
10. Algorithms Interview Questions You'll Most Likely Be Asked
11. Android Development Interview Questions You'll Most Likely Be Asked
12. Ant & Maven Interview Questions You'll Most Likely Be Asked
13. Apache Web Server Interview Questions You'll Most Likely Be Asked
14. Artificial Intelligence Interview Questions You'll Most Likely Be Asked
15. ASP.NET Interview Questions You'll Most Likely Be Asked
16. Automated Software Testing Interview Questions You'll Most Likely Be Asked
17. Base SAS Interview Questions You'll Most Likely Be Asked
18. BEA WebLogic Server Interview Questions You'll Most Likely Be Asked
19. C & C++ Interview Questions You'll Most Likely Be Asked
20. C# Interview Questions You'll Most Likely Be Asked
21. CCNA Interview Questions You'll Most Likely Be Asked
22. Cloud Computing Interview Questions You'll Most Likely Be Asked
23. Computer Architecture Interview Questions You'll Most Likely Be Asked
24. Computer Networks Interview Questions You'll Most Likely Be Asked
25. Core JAVA Interview Questions You'll Most Likely Be Asked
26. Data Structures & Algorithms Interview Questions You'll Most Likely Be Asked
27. EJB 3.0 Interview Questions You'll Most Likely Be Asked
28. Entity Framework Interview Questions You'll Most Likely Be Asked
29. Fedora & RHEL Interview Questions You'll Most Likely Be Asked
30. Hadoop BIG DATA Interview Questions You'll Most Likely Be Asked
31. Hibernate, Spring & Struts Interview Questions You'll Most Likely Be Asked
32. HR Interview Questions You'll Most Likely Be Asked
33. HTML, XHTML and CSS Interview Questions You'll Most Likely Be Asked
34. HTML5 Interview Questions You'll Most Likely Be Asked
35. IBM WebSphere Application Server Interview Questions You'll Most Likely Be Asked
36. Innovative Interview Questions You'll Most Likely Be Asked
37. iOS SDK Interview Questions You'll Most Likely Be Asked
38. Java / J2EE Design Patterns Interview Questions You'll Most Likely Be Asked
39. Java / J2EE Interview Questions You'll Most Likely Be Asked
40. JavaScript Interview Questions You'll Most Likely Be Asked
41. JavaServer Faces Interview Questions You'll Most Likely Be Asked
42. JDBC Interview Questions You'll Most Likely Be Asked
43. jQuery Interview Questions You'll Most Likely Be Asked
44. JSP-Servlet Interview Questions You'll Most Likely Be Asked
45. JUnit Interview Questions You'll Most Likely Be Asked
46. Leadership Interview Questions You'll Most Likely Be Asked
47. Linux Interview Questions You'll Most Likely Be Asked
48. Linux System Administrator Interview Questions You'll Most Likely Be Asked

49. Mac OS X Lion Interview Questions You'll Most Likely Be Asked
50. Mac OS X Snow Leopard Interview Questions You'll Most Likely Be Asked
51. Microsoft Access Interview Questions You'll Most Likely Be Asked
52. Microsoft Powerpoint Interview Questions You'll Most Likely Be Asked
53. Microsoft Word Interview Questions You'll Most Likely Be Asked
54. MySQL Interview Questions You'll Most Likely Be Asked
55. Networking Interview Questions You'll Most Likely Be Asked
56. OOPS Interview Questions You'll Most Likely Be Asked
57. Operating Systems Interview Questions You'll Most Likely Be Asked
58. Oracle Database Administration Interview Questions You'll Most Likely Be Asked
59. Oracle E-Business Suite Interview Questions You'll Most Likely Be Asked
60. ORACLE PL/SQL Interview Questions You'll Most Likely Be Asked
61. Perl Programming Interview Questions You'll Most Likely Be Asked
62. PHP Interview Questions You'll Most Likely Be Asked
63. Python Interview Questions You'll Most Likely Be Asked
64. RESTful JAVA Web Services Interview Questions You'll Most Likely Be Asked
65. SAP HANA Interview Questions You'll Most Likely Be Asked
66. SAS Programming Guidelines Interview Questions You'll Most Likely Be Asked
67. Selenium Testing Tools Interview Questions You'll Most Likely Be Asked
68. Silverlight Interview Questions You'll Most Likely Be Asked
69. Software Repositories Interview Questions You'll Most Likely Be Asked
70. Software Testing Interview Questions You'll Most Likely Be Asked
71. SQL Server Interview Questions You'll Most Likely Be Asked
72. Tomcat Interview Questions You'll Most Likely Be Asked
73. UML Interview Questions You'll Most Likely Be Asked
74. Unix Interview Questions You'll Most Likely Be Asked
75. UNIX Shell Programming Interview Questions You'll Most Likely Be Asked
76. Windows Server 2008 R2 Interview Questions You'll Most Likely Be Asked
77. XLXP, XSLT, XPATH, XFORMS & XQuery Interview Questions You'll Most Likely Be Asked
78. XML Interview Questions You'll Most Likely Be Asked

For complete list visit

www.vibrantpublishers.com